The
Celery Juice Miracle

The
Celery Juice Miracle

70 JUICE AND SMOOTHIE RECIPES

Annie Willis

Racehorse Publishing

Disclaimer

The contents of this book are not intended as medical advice. Discuss with a health care professional any medical concerns you may have, which prescription medications you're taking, and how juicing can affect them. Celery allergies are surprisingly common and, if severe, can lead to anaphylactic shock. If you've never tried celery or may have had a reaction in the past, proceed with caution. Having a birch or mugwort pollen allergy puts you at a greater risk of being allergic to celery. Keep an eye out for common symptoms, such as itching and swelling of the lips, tongue, and throat.

Racehorse Publishing books may be purchased in bulk at special discounts for sales promotion, corporate gifts, fund-raising, or educational purposes. Special editions can also be created to specifications. For details, contact the Special Sales Department, Skyhorse Publishing, 307 West 36th Street, 11th Floor, New York, NY 10018 or info@skyhorsepublishing.com.

Racehorse Publishing™ is a pending trademark of Skyhorse Publishing, Inc.®, a Delaware corporation.

Visit our website at www.skyhorsepublishing.com.

10 9 8 7 6 5 4 3 2 1

Library of Congress Cataloging-in-Publication Data is available on file.

Cover design credit: Brian Peterson
Cover illustration credit: Getty Images
Interior photography: Photos used under license by Shutterstock.com

ISBN: 978-1-63158-599-9
Ebook ISBN: 978-1-63158-607-1

Printed in China

Table of Contents

Introduction

Celery is sweeping the nation, and for good reason! This humble vegetable has not only been adding flavor and crunch to our soups, dips, and snacks for ages, but it's also been quietly filling us up with vital nutrients. So it's about time celery's underappreciated stalks got the recognition they deserve. The vitamins, minerals, and antioxidants in celery can help you fight belly bloat, boost your energy, beautify your skin and hair, lower your blood pressure, reduce painful inflammation, keep your blood sugar in check, and so much more.

Are you ready to discover a happier, healthier you? It's easier than you think, and it all starts with (you guessed it!) a few modest stalks of celery. If you're picturing yourself nibbling on unsatisfying snacks of plain celery while your stomach rumbles, think again. This is no starvation diet. Instead, you'll be making the most of celery's many benefits in a way that fills you up and makes you feel great.

How, you ask? By enjoying the simple genius that is fresh, homemade juice. Juicing your celery allows you to pack several stalks' worth of nutrients into a single, conveniently drinkable serving. But while plenty of people believe that's the best thing you could do with a bunch of celery—turn it into 16 ounces of pure, nutrient-rich juice—you're going to do better.

That's where the 10-Day Celery-Powered Detox comes in.

In those ten days, you'll learn to use celery to your advantage by combining it with other nutritional powerhouses in a way that works for *you*. You'll introduce celery-based juice into your diet in small servings, giving your body time to adjust to the change. You'll also incorporate other healthy habits and balanced, protein-filled meals to support your body's natural detoxifying processes. But the best part is, you'll be able to fully customize the plan to your health needs and dietary preferences. With 70 juices and smoothies to choose from, you'll be on your way to a happier, healthier you. Discover the miracles celery has to offer with *The Celery Juice Miracle*.

PART 1

The Mighty Celery Stalk

Do you have fond memories of snacking on "ants on a log" as a child? Or not-so-fond memories of chewing your way through hunger pangs the last time you were on a diet? Maybe you use celery to put some crunch in those creamy summer salads your family loves. If you're like most people, you probably use celery as a vehicle for tastier things: ranch dressing, peanut butter, or lemony hummus.

Before celery became the next big health craze, you probably didn't spend a lot of time thinking about it. The light green stalks don't exactly stand out in the produce section. As vegetables go, celery isn't especially flavorful. Even the most polarizing thing about it—its stringy texture—isn't terrible. People who don't love celery will probably still eat it under the right circumstances. In other words, celery is practical. It fades into the background of our everyday lives.

But now, we're rediscovering the truth: that this unassuming vegetable has been part of our collective history for millennia for good reason. From clearing your skin and revving your energy to protecting your heart and reducing your risk of certain cancers, celery can do it all. Let it take center stage in your diet and it may just transform your health!

Celery 101

Celery, or *Apium graveolens*, is a member of the carrot family, Apiaceae, along with anise, caraway, cilantro, cumin, dill, fennel, parsley, and parsnips (plus their more nefarious relative, poison hemlock). If you're one of the people fondly remembering their childhood snack of "ants on a log," you might think of celery as a classic American staple. But celery, which is originally from the Mediterranean Basin, is grown and eaten all over the world in various forms. In fact, the name "celery," which was first written in English in 1664, comes from the French *céleri*.

There, in Europe, you're likely to encounter a variety called celeriac, which is used for its bulb and leaves rather than its stalks. Asia boasts the oldest variety of celery: leaf celery, which is wispier and more strongly flavored than American celery. Wild celery, native to South America, is used for its leaves and seeds all over the world. In the United States, we tend to favor the crisp stalks and fragrant seeds over the leaves. No matter where in the world you go, the celery plant is often mistaken for just another mundane part of a larger culinary creation. But that's not at all how celery's journey began.

CELERY'S WILD PAST

The ancient Greeks considered celery anything but mundane. Instead of consuming wild celery, with its thin stalks and bitter flavor, they used it as an aphrodisiac, a crown of athletic victory, and a burial wreath. Its association with death was so strong at the time that the Greeks developed a catchphrase for when all hope of recovery was lost: "He now has need of nothing but celery."

The Greeks also associated celery with the other side of the eternal coin: vitality. Homer's renowned *Iliad* and *Odyssey* both make mention of it. In the *Iliad*, the horses of the Myrmidons graze on wild celery. In the *Odyssey*, the nymph Calypso's home enchanted Hermes with channels of water running through beds of it. Think about that: celery earned a place in literature that's nearly three millennia old and still read today!

In fact, respect for celery ran through all of the ancient civilizations, including ancient Rome, Egypt, and China. In addition to using it for celebrations and burials (archeologists found a wreath of celery in the tomb of Tutankhamun), these civilizations used the plant medicinally. They treated everything from common complaints, such as hangovers, to chronic conditions, such as arthritis.

These ancient civilizations seemed to understand something modern society is only now discovering—the hidden power of this seemingly unremarkable plant. It wasn't until Europeans began cultivating celery in the 1600s that people started taking it for granted as a filler food. And who could blame them? They needed something to make their meals go farther and feed more people, and celery fit the bill. Little did they know they were also benefiting from a deep well of nutrients!

COMING TO AMERICA

Celery owes its place in American supermarkets to a Scotsman named George Taylor, who took a chance on planting celery seeds from home in a place that had never heard of the vegetable—his new home of Kalamazoo, Michigan. In an effort to gain exposure, George offered to provide free celery to a local hotel for its banquet. It was a savvy business move that would help Kalamazoo become known as "Celery City," the starting point for the national celery market. Dutch immigrants soon poured into Michigan and began planting hundreds of acres of this popular new vegetable.

But celery wouldn't reach the masses right away. At first, it was expensive to cultivate and therefore its use was mostly ornamental. The wealthy displayed celery in special vases on their dining tables. It was also white, thanks to farmers shielding it from the sun to help suppress its bitterness. As cultivation evolved and production grew cheaper, celery became a grocery store staple. We can thank the pest problems and pricey production of the white varieties for the nutrient-rich green varieties we enjoy today.

CELERY GOES MAINSTREAM

Although celery is incredibly common now, there were several times in its American history when it was actually considered a novelty. Some celery-inspired concepts were successful, others less so. But with its renewed surge in popularity and our greater understanding of its health benefits, who knows how many amazing celery creations we can look forward to!

An Early Attempt at Green Juice

Before an Atlanta pharmacist created Coca-Cola, a mysterious Dr. Brown created a carbonated celery-based tonic (made with the seeds, not the stalks) to soothe the stomachs of his clients. In 1886, during the height of American interest in celery, he began to market his creation. He called it "Cel-Ray," due to the Food and Drug Administration's objection to use of the word "tonic." Eventually, Dr. Brown's Cel-Ray Soda found a home in New York delis, where you can still find it today. It may not be as good for you as green juice, but Dr. Brown deserves credit for trying to bring the health benefits of celery to the masses early on.

An American Icon

The 1950s and '60s were a time for experimentation—especially in the kitchen, where convenience was beginning to become a priority. This was the heyday for Jell-O molds, which became the trendy centerpiece for dinner parties and family gatherings. People began submerging all sorts of things in gelatin, from lamb chops to complete salads. Jell-O took note and developed three flavors geared toward the latter: Mixed Vegetable, Seasoned Tomato, and (of course) Celery. Thankfully, they realized their real calling was fruit-flavored dessert cups and left salads alone.

A Handy Utensil

You're probably familiar with celery's favorite cocktail, the Bloody Mary. The tomato-based beverage started out as the Oyster Cocktail in 1892, but by the 1950s, it had almost become the brunch favorite and hangover cure we know today. It awaited just one small finishing touch—the iconic celery stick garnish. We can thank the actions of a random customer for this much-needed alkaline addition, which balances out the acidity of the drink and gives you something nutritious to munch on in between sips. Said customer needed something to stir his drink and, not finding a spoon, reached for a celery stalk instead.

The Many Benefits of Celery

Celery may not be an instant panacea, but the tremendous nutritional content in each little 6-calorie stalk makes it a smart addition to your diet. Studies show that this mighty vegetable helps protect your heart, strengthen your bones, support your digestion, and enhance your brain function while fighting against the inflammation and oxidative stress that can lead to chronic illness and even certain types of cancer. But what is it, exactly, about this inconspicuous vegetable that makes it capable of all that? The answer: a powerful combination of antioxidants, vitamins, minerals, and phytonutrients that your body needs to do its best work.

ANTIOXIDANTS

You know that antioxidants are good for you. After all, it's mentioned on the labels of everything from breakfast cereal to face moisturizer. But do you know *why* antioxidants are good for you? In short, they can stop or delay damage to your cells done by free radicals. And celery happens to have more than a dozen antioxidants in a single stalk!

Free radicals are unstable atoms that can come from anywhere (outside toxins or even your own metabolism), attach to healthy cells, and cause damage, known as *oxidative stress*. And that damage can lead to signs of aging, inflammation, chronic illness, and even certain types of cancer. Although your body has natural ways to fend off free radicals, it needs all the help it can get. That's where antioxidants come in. They bind to these free radicals so that the harmful compounds are no longer free to bind to healthy cells and cause problems.

Now you're probably wondering how you can get your hands on some of these cancer-fighting compounds. The best source is the food you eat every day. Antioxidants are found in foods in the forms of vitamins A, C, and E as well as selenium, lutein, and lycopene—all of which you can find in celery. Your own digestion releases them into your bloodstream to clean up any free radicals they come into contact with. Juicing celery with other antioxidant-rich foods (such as berries, beets, and spinach) is a great way to fend off free radicals and preserve cellular health.

VITAMINS

Our bodies need vitamins in order to not just thrive, but to function at all. They strengthen our bones, heal our wounds, shore up our immune system, and keep our hearts pumping and our brains humming. They give us the energy to get up every morning and tackle a new day. But our bodies can't make vitamins. Instead, they're acquired through eating nutrient-rich fruits and veggies like celery. So, adding a celery-based green juice to your routine is an easy and enjoyable way to help you get more of the vitamins your body needs.

Vitamin A

A single serving of celery (two stalks) contains 10 percent of the FDA's recommended Daily Value (DV) of vitamin A, which is essential for good vision, immune health, and cell growth. The vitamin A you get from celery actually comes from the antioxidant beta-carotene, which gives you even more benefits than you get from the vitamin A in animal protein. Studies have shown that beta-carotene can slow cognitive decline, prevent skin damage, and help reduce or prevent the kind of cell damage that can lead to certain types of cancer. To get the most out of the vitamin A in your celery juice, pair it with a healthy fat (a handful of almonds, for example), which will help your body absorb it.

Vitamin C

Vitamin C is a powerhouse of a nutrient, helping to bolster your immune system, protect your heart, prevent eye disease, and even reduce wrinkles. It's also vital to the healing process and the formation of blood vessels, cartilage, muscle, and collagen in bones. And if that's not enough, vitamin C's antioxidant properties help it fight the free radicals that cause cell damage. A serving of celery (which is just two stalks) contains 6 percent of your recommended Daily Value. Combine it with other vitamin-rich fruits and veggies in a green juice, and you should be well on your way to hitting that target and feeling great.

Vitamin K

A single serving of celery packs a whopping 40 percent of your recommended Daily Value of vitamin K, which is essential for blood clotting and bone health. Studies have also shown that vitamin K benefits cognitive function, lowers blood pressure, and reduces the risks of heart disease and stroke. And if that doesn't already have you reaching for some celery juice, vitamin K is also used to speed healing and reduce redness, bruising, scars, stretch marks, and burns on the skin.

B Vitamins

If you've ever looked at the back of a bottle of multivitamins, you may have noticed a fair number of B vitamins. These are vital to your energy levels, brain function, and cell metabolism. Celery naturally contains seven out of the eight that you'll find listed in most supplements. While they all help your body convert food into energy, each one has its own role to play in your overall health.

- **Vitamin B$_1$ (thiamine).** Thiamine is essential for glucose metabolism (which helps you regulate your energy and blood sugar) as well as heart, muscle, and nerve function.
- **Vitamin B$_2$ (riboflavin).** In addition to using its antioxidant properties to prevent cell damage, riboflavin helps your body build red blood cells. Studies also show that taking it regularly may help prevent cataracts and migraines.
- **Vitamin B$_3$ (niacin).** Like other B vitamins, niacin helps your body covert nutrients into energy. But it may also help lower cholesterol, prevent heart disease, treat type 1 diabetes, protect skin cells, ease arthritis, and boost cognitive function.
- **Vitamin B$_5$ (pantothenic acid).** Pantothenic acid is essential for making blood cells, but it's also been studied as a treatment for everything from acne to neuralgia.
- **Vitamin B$_6$ (pyridoxine).** Vitamin B$_6$ is another multitasker that may help treat depression, improve cognitive function, reduce the risk of heart disease, maintain eye health, ease arthritis, and prevent certain types of cancer.
- **Vitamin B$_9$ (folate).** One serving of celery contains 10 percent of your recommended Daily Value of folate, which is responsible for making DNA and other genetic material. Studies show that getting enough folate can reduce your risk of cancer, depression, heart disease, stroke, and dementia.
- **Vitamin B$_{12}$ (cobalamin).** Like other B vitamins, vitamin B$_{12}$ is responsible for helping your body form red blood cells, but it may also support bone health, reduce your risks of macular degeneration and heart disease, boost your mood and your energy levels, improve cognitive function, and support healthy skin, hair, and nails.

All in all, B vitamins are incredibly important to your health and well-being. To make a blend rich in these essential nutrients, combine celery juice with some citrus fruits and dark, leafy vegetables.

MINERALS

Minerals are essential nutrients, meaning that your body can't function properly without the right amounts. "The right amounts" differ depending on which of two groups the mineral falls into: macrominerals or microminerals. As you probably guessed, your body needs larger amounts of macrominerals (calcium, magnesium, phosphorus, potassium, and sodium) and trace amounts of microminerals (copper, iron, manganese, selenium, and zinc). Each one of these minerals performs its own set of necessary functions. And once again, celery proves that it has more than meets the eye with a full profile of vital minerals.

Calcium

If you were ever lectured to drink your milk as a kid, you know that calcium helps build strong bones and teeth. But you may not know that calcium is also essential to muscle contraction, nerve impulse transmission, and blood vessel function. That's why getting enough of it is as important for adults as it is for children. Celery can help with 4 percent of your recommended Daily Value per serving. So, you can serve up that same nutritional wisdom to the little ones in your life with a glass of milk *and* a super-nutritious snack of "ants on a log."

Magnesium

Your body needs magnesium for more than 300 biochemical reactions. It supports nerve and muscle function, a regular heartbeat, a healthy immune system, and bone strength while regulating blood glucose levels and contributing to energy production. And some studies suggest that increasing your magnesium intake can help you manage migraines.

Phosphorus

Like calcium, phosphorus is essential for bone health. More specifically, it's vital for the growth, maintenance, and repair of cells and tissue and the production of both DNA and RNA (your genetic building blocks). Phosphorus also helps your body produce energy, your heart beat regularly, your kidneys filter out waste, and your muscles move.

Potassium

A single serving of celery contains 8 percent of your recommended Daily Value of potassium, which conducts electricity in the body and supports heart health, digestion, and muscular function. That puts it on par with bananas—the food most people reach for to boost their potassium levels—which offer 9 percent per serving.

Sodium
While we're often taught that sodium is a bad thing, it's actually an essential nutrient—in the right quantities. It's vital to nerve and muscle function, maintains the balance of water in and around your cells, and helps regulate your blood pressure and blood volume. Drinking celery juice is a great way to nourish your whole body while getting your recommended Daily Value.

Copper
Your body uses copper to support your immune system, make red blood cells, and maintain nerve cells. Studies show that it may also help protect you from arthritis, high blood pressure, high cholesterol, and osteoporosis.

Iron
Iron is a crucial component of hemoglobin, the substance in red blood cells that carries oxygen from your lungs to the rest of your body. Because iron is a micromineral, your body doesn't need much to get its fill. Adding celery to your diet is a good start!

Manganese
A serving of celery contains 6 percent of your recommended Daily Value of manganese, which your body needs for your brain, nervous system, and enzyme systems to function. It also helps your body metabolize other nutrients while regulating blood sugar, reducing inflammation, and protecting against oxidative stress.

Selenium
Selenium plays a role in metabolism, immune health, and thyroid function. But this mineral also has antioxidant properties that protect you from the oxidative stress that can cause heart disease, cognitive decline, and even certain types of cancer. Plus, studies show that selenium may help reduce asthma symptoms.

Zinc
Zinc is a multivitamin staple that's essential to your immune health, helping your body fight off harmful bacteria and viruses. Your body also uses it in the processes of DNA synthesis, digestion, wound healing, and metabolism. New research suggests that zinc may also play a role in your ability to concentrate, so a glass of celery-based green juice might come in handy to revive you during a long day at work or school.

PHYTONUTRIENTS

Every study of plant-rich diets demonstrates that people who eat more plants have fewer serious health problems. Scientists believe we have phytonutrients to thank for that, though they're still figuring out how exactly phytonutrients work. What they do know is that phytonutrients (which are also called phytochemicals) are chemicals produced by plants to help them stay healthy. And luckily for us, those beneficial properties transfer to anyone who eats the plants that contain them!

Some phytonutrients act the same way that antioxidants do, attaching themselves to free radicals and protecting our healthy cells from damage. Others help support the actions of antioxidants. But perhaps the most important role of phytonutrients is their effect on inflammation. More and more studies show that inflammation can lead to serious illness, such as heart disease and certain types of cancer. Eating a diet that's consistently rich in phytonutrients like those found in celery may help reduce inflammation and prevent its detrimental effects.

FLAVONOIDS

Flavonoids are technically a subset of phytonutrients—the largest one, in fact—but their benefits deserve their own spotlight. These plant chemicals have powerful anti-inflammatory, cancer-fighting, and immune-boosting properties that can help your body fight off everything from the common cold to certain types of cancer.

Some of the notable flavonoids in celery are the flavones apigenin and luteolin and the flavonol quercetin. Like other antioxidants, apigenin and luteolin both help combat the cell damage (oxidative stress) that can lead to signs of aging, chronic illness, and certain types of cancer. But luteolin may actually fight cancer, itself—it's been shown to kill human pancreatic cancer cells in laboratory tests. Both flavones also protect your body from the inflammation that can cause arthritis, heart disease, cognitive decline, and digestive disorders such as gastritis.

Quercetin has formidable anti-inflammatory and antioxidant properties, too, but its benefits don't stop there. It also has antibacterial and antihistamine properties that help it prevent skin, stomach, respiratory, and urinary infections as well as hay fever and hives. If you're an allergy sufferer, make sure you add a blend of celery and quercetin-rich apples to your routine!

POLYSACCHARIDES

Contrary to popular belief, not all sugars are bad for you. Pectin, a natural fiber found in most plants (including celery), is a long-chain sugar, or polysaccharide. Studies show that pectin can help treat digestive issues, lower cholesterol, fight diabetes, and support weight loss. Research also suggests that the pectin-based polysaccharide apiuman, in particular, may help reduce the risk of gastric ulcers by improving the stomach lining and regulating stomach secretions. One of the best sources of pectin is the skin of a fruit or vegetable, which is why it's important to eat whole produce in addition to using peeled produce in your juices.

CARBOHYDRATES

Many of us have been trained by fad diets to think that carbohydrates are inherently bad. But did you know that fiber is a carbohydrate? And no one can say that getting enough fiber is a bad thing. Not only does it help regulate your digestion, but studies show that it may also reduce your risk of developing breast cancer, diabetes, diverticular disease, and heart disease. A single serving of celery contains 7 percent of your recommended Daily Value of fiber. But the trick is that you have to eat the vegetable whole or blend it into a smoothie without straining it to get most of that fiber. Again, that's why maximizing your wellness means balancing healthy juicing habits with healthy eating habits.

Sugar is another carbohydrate that gets a bad rap because it can be too easy for people to overindulge. But your body does need some sugar to survive. It just doesn't need any *added* sugar. The complex carbohydrates that the body converts into sugar combined with the sugar that naturally occurs in healthy foods gives you more than you need. Still, if you're watching your sugar, you'll want to stick to low-glycemic juice blends.

WATER CONTENT

Another one of celery's many benefits is that its stalks are approximately 95 percent water. Yes, that means that all of those nutrients are packed into just 5 percent of the vegetable! But it also means that celery is both a low-calorie snack *and* one of the most hydrating things you can eat.

Proper hydration can help you eliminate toxins, prevent illness, regulate your weight, improve your skin, increase your energy levels, boost brain function, put you in a better mood, and even reduce your risk of heart attack. Your body and all of its functions depend on it, and too many people don't get enough of it in a day. But juicing makes staying hydrated tasty and convenient. Start any blend with celery, and you're already better off.

ALKALINITY

Although alkalinity is not a nutrient, it is an important health benefit. Celery happens to be one of the most alkaline foods available, but eating it can do more than just combat heartburn and acid reflux. It can also help bring your body's pH back into balance.

If you're new to nutrition, you may not realize how important pH is to your health. The human body is all about balance. It runs best at its natural pH of 7.4 and always tries to return to that number, improvising solutions whenever it runs too acidic or too alkaline. But it needs your help. The foods you eat have a huge impact on your body's pH, and most people tend toward acidic diets. (Acidic foods include meat, white sugar, chocolate, coffee, and potatoes, so you can see why.) But illness and disease thrive in acidic environments.

To help your body find its balance, you want to make sure your diet is 70 percent alkaline and only 30 percent acidic. But here's the tricky part: a food's own pH has little to do with how it affects your body's pH. For example, lemons are acidic, but they have an alkaline effect on the body. Here are a few more foods to get you started in finding your balance:

ACIDIC	ALKALINE
Artificial sweeteners	Garlic
Blueberries	Goat cheese
Beef	Grapefruit
Butter	Green tea
Chicken	Maple syrup
Eggs	Olive oil
Pasta	Raw honey
Peanuts	Sweet potatoes
Oats	Tomatoes
String beans	Watermelon

The Bottom Line

After getting to know celery's nutritional profile, it's easy to see why some people think that celery juice is the magic pill they've been searching for. Little did you know that this unassuming vegetable had hidden depths of vitamins and nutrients and such a long history of helping people.

Not all of its nutritional numbers are large, but you wouldn't want them to be. Consuming large quantities of certain vitamins and minerals can cause more health problems than it would prevent. And celery's ability to complement other delicious fruits and veggies in both flavor and nutritional value is part of its charm. It's the perfect nutrient boost when added to a well-rounded diet!

If the idea of "a well-rounded diet" sounds like torture to you, just wait until you've tried the just wait until you've tried the 10-Day Celery-Powered Detox outlined in Part 3. You'll find that celery-based juices are a yummy treat you look forward to. And because they retrain your sweet tooth, you'll be less likely to crave all those sugary, acidic, inflammation-causing foods your body's used to (and suffering from). Once you learn how to get the most out of your detox, you'll be well on your way to the good health you deserve!

PART 2

Making the Most of Your Celery

The happier, healthier version of you is just ten days away! As you know by now, the 10-Day Celery-Powered Detox is not your ordinary get-slim-quick cleanse. You don't want to drop ten pounds in a week just to gain them back. And you know that starving yourself for ten days isn't going to make you feel good. You need a plan. A plan that will work for you not just in the short term but also for the long haul. A plan that will train you to fuel your body for a lifetime of feeling good and looking great. That's what the 10-Day Celery-Powered Detox is: a customizable plan to help you transform your health.

But learning how to get the most out of those first ten celery-filled days can make all the difference in your success following them. You thought there was nothing to it, right? Throw some celery into a juicer and enjoy your freshly homemade juice? Not quite. You need to know how to choose the right ingredients, make the best blends, and prep your produce, not to mention getting the hang of the whole juicing process itself. (Don't worry—it's easy!) Once you do, you'll be able to maximize your celery-based blends for both flavor and nutrition.

A Quick Note on Terminology

While getting clear on the terminology surrounding celery isn't incredibly important, it can be really helpful. Bunch, head, stalk, rib, stick, branch—what does it all mean? Well, that depends on whom you ask. Technically speaking, "bunch," "head," and "stalk" all mean the same thing: a whole celery plant. "Rib" is the correct term for one piece (or stick or branch) of celery. Confused yet?

That's probably because the technical terminology has long since given way to common usage. To most people, the package of celery you buy at the store is a "bunch," and a single piece of celery is a "stalk." Those are the terms you'll see throughout this book. So, if a recipe calls for two stalks (as many of them do), you can rest assured it doesn't mean two whole heads of celery.

But you'll still need to be mindful of the terminology once you leave the comfort of these pages and head out on your own juicing journey. Some recipe writers are sticklers, and some have no idea which end of a celery stalk is up. Context is key when following new recipes. Check the number of servings and how much other produce is listed. If a recipe makes one serving of juice and calls for one apple, one cucumber, and a "bunch" of celery, the recipe writer probably wants you to add a handful of chopped celery. Of course, if you can't figure out amounts from context, you can always taste the juice and correct from there. Juicing mistakes are easily fixed!

Choosing Your Celery

Before today, you only thought you knew how to buy celery. You may be used to grabbing the first bunch you see at the store, but you'll want to be a little more thoughtful when it comes to the produce you buy for your juice blends. Seemingly small things can make a big difference.

When you're using celery in your cooking, the quality of the celery matters a little less. That's because you're heating the celery to a temperature that changes its texture and flavor and destroys any potentially harmful bacteria or chemicals. When you're juicing your celery or eating it raw, you only want the best!

FRESHNESS

Freshness is important first and foremost because you want to maximize the amount of nutrients in your celery. The closer to harvest a fruit or vegetable is, the more nutrients it has. As time passes, more nutrients are lost. Look for celery that's a bright light green, compact (the stalks are tightly packed), crisp, and smells fresh and slightly spicy. Once you get your celery home, the stalks should easily snap off the base when pulled. Celery that's past its prime will have thinner stalks that fall limply apart and may smell "off." Avoid bunches with stalks that are white or discolored, soft, or bendable.

FARMING

You might think that "organic" is just a fancy way of saying "expensive," but when it comes to celery juice, the designation really does matter. Organic produce comes from farms that have earned the hard-won United States Department of Agriculture (USDA) Organic Seal. To do that, they have to adhere to stringent production and labeling standards. And the USDA takes the designation very seriously. (People who knowingly label a nonorganic product as organic can be fined up to $17,952 for each violation!)

What "Organic" Means

The farming practices that the USDA requires for an Organic Seal are designed to enhance soil and water quality, reduce pollution, and essentially optimize the health and productivity of the plants and animals being farmed. These farmers work *with* nature to do what's best for the plant and its environment. Conventional farms, on the other hand, might try to churn out as much produce as possible as quickly as possible, sometimes to the detriment of the produce and the people eating it. Buying organic means you're doing what's healthy for you *and* the planet.

Pesticide Problems

Supporting farmers who respect and nourish the environment is always a good thing to do, but buying organic is also the smart thing to do when your goal is to turn raw produce into nutritious juice. Studies show that organic produce contains more nutrients, lower amounts of toxic metals (which can be absorbed through the soil), and lower levels of pesticides than conventionally grown produce.

Pesticide residue is your biggest concern when it comes to eating raw produce. Exposure to pesticides has been linked to serious health issues such as fertility problems, respiratory illness, neurological disorders, and even certain cancers. That's why, every year, the Environmental Working Group (EWG) puts out two lists: the Dirty Dozen and the Clean Fifteen. Those items with the highest concentrations of harmful chemicals are placed on the Dirty Dozen list, and people are encouraged to buy only their organic counterparts. Unfortunately, nonorganic celery makes this list every year.

That's not to say that you can't buy conventionally farmed celery. You can—and should—wash all of your produce to reduce your exposure to any pesticides or harmful bacteria. But when you're consuming large amounts of any type of produce, you want to make sure you're only putting good things into your body.

Grow Your Own

Do you want to know for sure that your celery is fresh and clean? Grow your own! It's easy to grow, and you'll be able to harvest it right from your own garden for every recipe. You can even give your celery a head start by using the base of your last celery bunch instead of seeds. Simply place the cut base in a small bowl of water on a sunny windowsill and watch it sprout roots and stalks. Then move it to your garden, bury the roots and base with soil, water it well, and watch it grow. Do this with a few bunches and you'll have plenty of fresh, organic celery to pluck from!

PACKAGING

When you walk into the produce section of most stores, you're going to find a few celery options. There's the conventionally farmed celery and the organic celery, which may be in bags or simply bound. And then there's the pre-washed and -cut celery in its plastic packaging, which may or may not be organic. And each of these options might offer another choice of leaves or no leaves. Who knew that choosing celery could be so complicated? (Don't worry—it isn't!)

Costly Convenience

You already know enough to walk past the conventionally farmed celery. If you're in a hurry or just a fan of convenience, you might reach for the (organic) precut produce. Just keep in mind that the precut celery is often more expensive, and that's on top of the premium you're paying for organic produce. Plus, the package may contain less than a full bunch, requiring you to buy even more of it. And here's the kicker: cut celery loses nutrients more quickly than whole celery. That's why your best bet is usually untrimmed bunches of organic celery.

Keep the Leaves

Whether you buy your celery precut or whole, make sure it includes the leaves. Juicing can eliminate some of the nutrients found in produce because you need to remove the skins, cores, or seeds, where nutrients are stored. But celery leaves, which contain a lot of the plant's calcium, potassium, and vitamin C, can be juiced right alongside their stalks. So, keeping the leaves can be an easy way to boost your nutrients.

Or Don't Keep the Leaves

Using celery leaves can affect the flavor of the juice, and not everyone's a fan. Some people think juicing the leaves makes their blends bitter, but you can decide for yourself. Try making the same juice recipe with and without the leaves to see which you like better. You can always add a splash of lemon juice to balance out the flavor of the leaves, but don't feel guilty about excluding the leaves if you don't like them. Remember: developing healthy habits is all about making them work for you. And some nutrients are better than none!

QUANTITY

So now the question is how much to buy. In your excitement to start feeling the benefits of celery juice, you might be tempted to fill your cart. How much celery you need to buy will generally depend on which recipes you plan on using, but a couple of bunches per week should be all you need. A full bunch (or head) of celery will usually contain sixteen stalks. Each stalk produces about 1 ounce of juice, so a bunch of celery will make about 16 ounces. Because you'll be maximizing celery's effects by combining it with other fruits and vegetables, you shouldn't need to buy a ton of it. (But grab an extra bunch if you like your juice heavy on the celery.)

Storing Your Celery

You already know that produce begins to lose nutrients from the moment farmers harvest it. And you know that the first step in stemming the loss is to buy the freshest celery you can find. The next step is to store your celery properly, and that starts with getting rid of any plastic wrappers or packages. Veggies need air circulation to keep them fresh, and plastic can suffocate them. Instead, wrap your celery snugly with aluminum foil but don't crimp the ends of the foil. This will protect it from moisture loss while allowing it to breathe.

GIVE IT SPACE
Your foil-wrapped celery should be stored in the refrigerator. While you may be tempted to throw all of your juicing ingredients into the crisper drawer, it's important to separate your fruits and veggies. Fruits produce ethylene gas, which is a ripening agent that can speed spoilage. Celery is particularly sensitive to ethylene, so keep it in the crisper with other vegetables and find the fruits a home elsewhere in the fridge.

CLEAN IT LATER
Another trick to maintain freshness is to store your celery unwashed and untrimmed. When you wash produce before you store it, the remaining moisture can encourage bacterial growth and spoilage. Plus, cutting celery causes the clock to tick faster on those nutrients. Instead, wash and cut your produce just before you use it. A little extra moisture certainly won't hurt the juice!

REVIVE SAD STALKS
If your celery starts to look a little limp during storage, submerge the stalks in water in the refrigerator for a couple of hours. They'll absorb the water and perk up. This is also a good way to store cut stalks (if you cut more than you need, for example): place them in the refrigerator in an airtight container filled with water to help them retain their moisture, crisp texture, and nutrients.

USE IT UP
If you've followed all the guidelines for proper storage, your celery should keep for one to two weeks in the refrigerator. But remember that your celery is losing more nutrients every day. If you have a store nearby, it might be worth the extra trip to buy one bunch at

a time and enjoy the extra nutrients. Aim to use up your celery within five to seven days, and your celery leaves (which are more fragile) within two.

If it turns out that you bought more celery than you can use in that amount of time, you can actually freeze the excess. There are two ways to do it:

- **Blanched.** Blanching the celery can preserve its flavor and make it last longer—up to a year and a half—in the freezer but can result in losing more than a third of its nutrients. To use this method, first wash and cut the celery. Then blanch it by dropping it into boiling water, letting it cook for 3 minutes, and then plunge it into ice water to stop the cooking process. Finally, pat the celery dry before storing it in an airtight container in the freezer.
- **Not blanched.** You can skip the blanching part of the process above and freeze the celery for up to a few months. You may lose some of the flavor, but you'll maintain the nutrients.
- In either case, the celery will be a bit soft when it thaws. It wouldn't be good for a crunchy snack, but it'll still be perfect for celery juice.

Preparing Your Celery

Prepping your celery for juicing is quick and easy. First, check your recipe for how many stalks of celery you'll need. If you're only using a few:

1. Snap the stalks off from the root of the bunch.
2. Re-wrap the remaining bunch and return it to the refrigerator.
3. Run the stalks under cold water, using your hands or a produce brush to remove any dirt or residue. (If you're using nonorganic celery, make sure you wash the stalks more thoroughly, using your hands to firmly rub away any residue under the water.) Don't worry about drying your celery—a little extra hydration is never a bad thing.

4. Cut away the white bottom.
5. Cut off the leafy tops if you prefer not to use them or the recipe specifically says to leave them out.

If you're using the whole bunch, you can simply cut away the white root and leafy tops (optional) first so that you don't have to do it sixteen times. Then just wash the cut stalks before moving on to juicing.

Whether or not you chop up the celery stalks will depend on your juicing method. Some juicers require that you chop the celery; others can take stalks whole. If you're using a blender, you'll need to cut the celery into 2- to 3-inch pieces. Either way, make sure you wash your hands when you finish handling the celery. Celery juice left on the skin can cause photosensitivity (a bad reaction when exposed to the sun).

Juicing 101

You know that a diet that's heavy in plants is incredibly beneficial for your health. So, how many servings of fruits and vegetables do you eat in a day? Researchers recommend that you eat four servings of fruit and five servings of vegetables *every day*. Are you keeping up? If not, you're not alone! Packing in that much produce is hard. But it doesn't have to be. By adding juicing to your daily routine, you can squeeze all the nutrition of several servings into one delicious glass.

EASY DOES IT

If you're just beginning your journey to health and happiness, juicing is a great place to start. Because your digestive system is not used to so many servings of fruits and vegetables, it can be sensitive to the increase in fiber. But juicing eliminates most of the fiber, making it the best way to enjoy nutrient-rich plants without upsetting your stomach. Simply supplement your diet with juice while upping your intake of whole fruits and veggies for the perfect balance.

TEXTURE ISSUES

Is one of the reasons you're not eating enough fruits and veggies that you're not crazy about some of their textures? Juicing can fix that for you, too. Celery strings, apple skins, raspberry seeds—whatever it is that makes you squirm, it's not a problem with juice. If the juicing process doesn't strain it out, it still only spends a millisecond in your mouth. There's no chewing required.

THE BENEFITS

Juicing does so much more than ease you into a healthy diet. It infuses your body with countless nutritional benefits all by itself. Do it right, and adding celery juice to your diet will give you more energy, clearer skin, better digestion, a stronger immune system, and more focus and mental dexterity. It could also help you slim down, lower your blood pressure, and relieve illness-causing inflammation as well as help you kick sugar cravings and keep the rest of your diet on track.

Those are all the benefits of getting your recommended daily servings of fruits and veggies in one convenient and tasty little package. And those are all benefits you won't find in bottled juices at the grocery store. Packaged juices can have added sugars, and they definitely have less nutritional content. Heat from the pasteurization process kills beneficial enzymes, and that's before the juice is even bottled, warehoused, shipped, shelved, and sold. By juicing at home, you're ensuring that you're receiving the maximum benefits that fresh produce has to offer and you're taking control of your health.

Juicer or No Juicer

Now you're sold on juicing. So, how do you get started? Investing in a really great juicer may be a smart move, especially if you're committed to juicing for the long haul. But it's not a necessity. With a few extra steps, you can use the same high-speed blender you use for all of your culinary creations. Either way, you'll end up with a nutritious glass of celery juice and be well on your way to a happier, healthier you!

CHOOSING A JUICER

Think you're ready for a dedicated juicer? You don't need a fancy one to start making delicious celery juice, but it certainly helps eliminate some of the work. Selecting one may be the hardest part of adding healthy green juice to your wellness routine. With so many great juicers to choose from, you'll really need to think about how much you want to spend, what you want to accomplish, and what works for your lifestyle.

Consider Your Budget

You can find great options in just about any price range. And remember that you don't have to go all in on Day 1. You can start with a lower-priced model, get used to the whole idea of juicing, and then eventually invest in a better model. That way, you have time to figure out what you like and don't like in a juicer. On the other hand, investing in a pricier piece of machinery could be a good way to hold yourself accountable for using it. No matter what, do what works for you!

Get to Know High-Speed Juicers

Most juicers fall into one of two categories: centrifugal (or high-speed) juicers and masticating (or slow) juicers. Centrifugal juicers use centrifugal force to separate the juice from the pulp, similar to the way a washing machine spins clothes to remove water. These juicers are amazingly fast at producing juice, often from whole produce. They contain a spinning serrated blade that cuts the produce for you as you feed it in. The leftover pulp goes into a removable bin or basket that's easy to clean.

Their speed makes centrifugal juicers a time-saver on a busy morning, but it comes with a cost. These juicers are very loud, and they often don't extract as much juice as slow juicers do. Some models offer two speeds to help you get the most juice out of different types of produce. (For example, you can use the lower speed for citrus and the higher speed for apples.) This feature can help with a higher yield, but only by a bit. Centrifugal juicers also have a harder time juicing leafy greens and herbs. And because the produce is cut and spun at high speeds, the machine produces a lot of heat and excess air, which cause the nutrients to break down and the juice to spoil more quickly. You'll notice that the juice is dark and sometimes frothy, indicating that it's already started to oxidize when it leaves the machine.

Centrifugal juicers are a great option for those who are just starting out on their juicing journey, those who don't have a lot of time for juicing, and those who will make small batches of juice and enjoy it immediately. They're usually compact and inexpensive as well as easy to clean, with just a few removable parts. And they work well with hard fruits and thick veggies. They do limit your ability to get creative with your blends and to enjoy all of the available nutrients. But that may be a fine compromise if the convenience means that you'll actually use the juicer. Some nutrient-rich juice is better than no nutrient-rich juice!

Get to Know Slow Juicers

When it comes to maximizing the quantity and quality of your celery juice, masticating juicers have centrifugal juicers beat. These machines use a slowly rotating auger to crush produce against a stainless-steel mesh screen (like a meat grinder), which results in even more juice being pulled from the pulp. Masticating juicers can accommodate any kind of produce, from crunchy apples to nutrient-dense leaves of spinach and kale. And because the auger produces almost no heat, you get to enjoy more of those nutrients for longer. You'll also notice a lot less waste with a masticating juicer, which is important when you're paying a premium for quality produce.

But masticating juicers aren't without their faults. For one thing, using a masticating juicer is more time-consuming. Not only do they physically work more slowly than centrifugal juicers, but they also have a smaller chute and no blades, so you'll have to do more prep work. Because they use a fine-mesh screen to strain the juice, they can clog more easily. This requires you to stop, turn off the machine, take apart the auger, and clean the screen. And cleaning the machine's many moving parts can take up more time than the juicing process itself.

Masticating juicers are great for people who are ready to fully commit to making juicing a daily habit. If you can make a little extra time in your day and a little extra space on your countertops, you'll be rewarded with juice that's light, vibrant, and nutritious. Masticating juicers are also handy when you have a house full of people—they're so quiet that you'll be the only one in the house who knows you're juicing in the morning. And if juicing inspires you to make more homemade goodies, you can also use your masticating juicer to make fresh nut butters, sorbets, and even pastas as long as you have the right attachments.

Get to Know Triturating Juicers
Triturating juicers (also called "twin-gear" juicers) are a less common third option. Because they're very large, are on the pricier end of the spectrum, and require more prep and cleanup, they're often left to die-hard juicing devotees and commercial juice bars. If you start juicing and discover that you love it and can't live without your daily blends, you may eventually want to invest in a triturating juicer.

Much like masticating juicers, triturating juicers use augers to crush produce and press the juice out of it. But rather than one large auger, triturating juicers use two interlocking augers to crush the produce *between them* at a slower speed, which extracts even more juice (from every type of produce) than masticating juicers and helps it last longer. So while you need to drink juice made with a centrifugal juicer right away, and you need to drink the juice made with a masticating juicer within 48 hours, you can enjoy nutrient-rich juice from your twin-gear juicer for up to 72 hours.

Triturating juicers also have the same multifunctionality that masticating juicers have. With the right attachments, you can make nut butters, sorbets, pasta noodles, and more. That makes this a great option for people who fully embrace the holistic approach to health and want the versatility to control more of what goes into their bodies.

Keep the Cleanup in Mind

Once you've finished blending your juice and enjoying it, you'll need to clean the juicer. And juicing is a messy process (though, luckily, the mess is usually contained within the machine). Both centrifugal and masticating juicers require some elbow grease, but some models of each are easier to maintain than others. If you hate cleanup and having to hand-wash dishes, make sure you choose a model with parts that are easy to disassemble and dishwasher safe.

Pick One You Like

One last consideration in buying a juicer is its appearance. Are you going to be storing your juicer in plain sight, or will you tuck it away? If your juicer will be a fixture of your kitchen countertop, you'll want to choose one that you like the look of and that fits within the space you have. If it's going to live in a cabinet between uses, you'll want something more compact and easier to lift out a couple of times per day. This isn't a matter of vanity. You want this machine to work for the way you live—not the way you think you *should* live. If it doesn't, you're more likely to give up on juicing early on and let that expensive appliance collect dust. So pick a juicer you *like*!

USING YOUR JUICER

When you're first starting out on your juicing journey, the most important thing to do is make sure you're following all of the directions you're given. That includes both the manufacturer's instructions for your juicer and the recipe instructions for your first few blends. Once you get the hang of things, you can start to get creative with the recipes. But there's no getting creative with your juicer. Thoroughly following all manufacturer guidelines for your particular model is essential for keeping it in tip-top shape for years to come and getting the most out of your investment. You'll need to know:

- How to assemble your machine
- Where to place your juice and pulp receptacles
- Which types of produce you can and cannot juice
- How to prep your produce
- How to safely feed the produce into the machine
- How to clear any clogs
- How to clean the machine

Although a lot of this depends on your particular model, you can follow a few general tips and guidelines.

Corral the Mess

One quick way for that juicing mess to make it to your countertop is to put your containers in the wrong spot. No matter which type of juicer you have, you'll need a receptacle beneath the spout where the juice comes out. If you have a masticating juicer, you may also need a separate container beneath the augur, where the pulp comes out. Double-check whether your container is really where it needs to be before you start juicing.

Prep Your Produce

The very first thing you'll do with your produce is wash all of it using your hands or a produce brush. Don't worry about drying it—your juicer was made to handle moisture. It wasn't made to handle cores, pits, or large seeds, though. Make sure you remove these before juicing so you don't clog the machine. Peels aren't usually a problem for your juicer, though recipes may occasionally call for removing them because they can affect a blend's flavor. Citrus peels can also irritate the digestive system, so you are sometimes better off removing them before adding sections to your juicer.

Whether you chop up your produce will also depend on your particular model. Centrifugal juicers don't usually require it. The smaller chute on a masticating juicer might just mean using fewer stalks of celery at a time rather than chopping it up. But some vertical masticating juicers don't do well with whole produce at all. In particular, celery strings may catch on the auger and make it jam. That's why it's so important to read the directions for not just your type of juicer but also for your particular model of juicer.

Juice the Right Way

No matter which kind of juicer you use, make sure you don't overload it. Add one ingredient at a time and watch the centrifuge or auger to ensure that the produce is moving through the machine before adding more. Trying to stuff whole bunches of produce in to save time will only end up costing you more as you jam the machine and need to stop to clear it.

Want to know the trick to getting the most juice out of your produce, no matter which juicer you use? Alternate the order in which you feed your ingredients into the juicer between hard and soft pieces. The hard produce, such as carrots, will help push the soft produce, such as leafy greens, through the mechanism of the machine. The recipes in this book are written so that you can juice the ingredients in the order they're listed. But if you're using a centrifugal juicer that has a hard time with leafy greens, you can just sandwich them between your stalks of celery to help them get processed.

You might notice some foam on top of your finished juice, especially if you're using a centrifugal juicer. That's a combination of the machine whipping up the juice as it pushes it out and some of the fiber not making it into the pulp bin. If it bothers you, you can strain the foam. (Your model might come with a container that has a built-in strainer. If not, you can always use a fine-mesh strainer or sieve to remove any foam or excess pulp.) But it's also perfectly fine—and sometimes a little more nutritious—to just stir it into the juice!

Keep a Safe Distance

This part is incredibly important. Both centrifugal juicers and masticating juicers include plungers to help you push your produce down into the chute. **Do not use your hands to push in the produce.** And **don't** pull the pulp out of a masticating juicer while the machine is on. That puts your fingers far too close to the auger. If your masticating juicer becomes clogged or jammed, try using the reverse button or toggle to unclog it. If that doesn't work, turn the machine off before disassembling it to clean the clogged area. Remember: both centrifugal juicers and masticating juicers are powerful pieces of machinery that make quick work of hard produce. Don't let carelessness cost you your fingers!

Clean the Machine

Adding celery juice to your diet is all about giving yourself a much-needed nutritional boost. So, the last thing you want to do is let your juicer become a breeding ground for bacteria. The solution is simple: make sure you clean your machine well after every use. Even if you use the juicer in the morning and plan to make more juice in the afternoon, you need to clean that machine after your morning batch.

This may seem like a pain, but it actually makes your life easier. Instead of scrubbing hardened pulp from the sides of the juicer's reservoir, you can simply rinse it away before running a soapy sponge over it. Follow your model's instructions to make sure you get to every piece that needs cleaning. Then your juicer is refreshed and ready for your next batch, preserving the produce's flavor and nutrition.

CHOOSING A BLENDER

Not quite ready to run out and buy a dedicated juicer? No problem! You can make delicious celery juice in minutes with a good blender and an ordinary kitchen strainer. A dedicated juicer may help you maximize the nutrients in your juice, but a high-speed blender can simplify your juicing routine and make staying healthy more practical.

Multitasking appliances like blenders can save you money, space, and time. While you'll have to expend a little more effort to prep your produce, cleaning a blender is a snap compared to cleaning a juicer. The only caveat is that you'll need to consume your juice within a day to avoid losing too many nutrients. If you already own a blender you love, you're all set. But if you're in the market, you'll have lots of great options to consider.

Decide on a Budget

Just like juicers, blenders come in a range of sizes, styles, abilities, and prices. The best types for juicing are personal bullet-style blenders and high-performance blenders that specifically indicate they can handle juicing, but simple countertop blenders can get the job done in a pinch. The first thing to consider is what price you're comfortable paying. Although blenders can cost as much as (if not more than) juicers, they do serve multiple functions. Just keep in mind that the better the blender, the less pulp you'll need to strain out and the more fiber and nutrients you'll find in your juice. So, buying the best blender that you can afford will go a long way toward making the most of your new wellness routine.

Get to Know Bullet-Style Blenders

Personal bullet-style blenders are small blenders that make one or two servings of juice at a time. You use them by filling bullet-shaped plastic cups with your ingredients, topping the cup with a screw-on lid fitted with a blade, and then inverting the whole thing onto the base of the blender. Some of these have controls on the base while others require you to push down on the cup to pulse or blend at one preset speed.

These blenders often come with multiple styles of cups and lids so that your blending cup instantly becomes your drinking glass or to-go tumbler. This is a great option for smoothies, but for juices, you'll still need to strain the contents into another container before pouring the juice back into your to-go cup. All in all, this process still gives you one less piece to wash than other high-speed blenders. And cleanup is a breeze compared with dedicated juicers. You'll only need to wash the cup and the blade, which are usually both dishwasher friendly. Plus, if you get one that comes with multiple cups, you'll always have a clean one when you need it!

Bullet-style blenders are great for people who are juicing just for themselves, and for those who want to create different blends for multiple people. Unfortunately, they're no quieter than traditional blenders. But they are quick. Although most bullet-style blenders can handle juicing, look for one that's specifically optimized for it. These aren't much more money than regular bullet-style blenders, and they can help you extract more nutritional value from your produce.

Get to Know High-Performance Blenders

As the name suggests, high-performance blenders are some of the most efficient blenders you can buy. They make quick work of every type of produce, sometimes pureeing it so completely that you'll have little pulp to strain out. That means that you'll get more of the nutrients and digestion-revving fiber in your juice without the fibrous texture.

These professional-style blenders are still what you picture when you hear the word "blender": a classic pitcher with a blade in the bottom that rests in an electric base. But they offer a much larger range of functionality than a traditional blender, including varying speeds and even automatic presets for particular creations. Some also have timers, self-cleaning functions, and serving settings.

Though they tend to be on the larger side of countertop appliances, high-performance blenders still take up less space than most masticating juicers. They're also much easier to clean, often dishwasher safe, and can usually accommodate four servings or more. And they're a great appliance for multitasking, helping you create everything from soup to nut butters and even ice cream.

High-performance blenders are a great option for someone who likes to make a few servings of juice at once or someone who makes juice for the whole household. And because they produce nutrient-dense juice, they're perfect for making the most of your 10-Day Celery-Powered Detox. The best part is, high-performance blenders start at the same low price as bullet-style blenders. Just make sure you choose one that offers 800 watts or more of blending power to ensure maximum nutrition.

Get to Know Traditional Countertop Blenders

If you're just starting out and you're not sure this whole juicing thing is for you, a traditional, inexpensive blender can help you figure it out. You won't enjoy the full spectrum of nutrients that you would get from a dedicated juicer or a high-speed blender, but you'll get an idea of how much effort goes into juicing, whether it's something you can fit into your lifestyle, and whether you like the taste of green juice enough to drink it daily. Like high-speed blenders, traditional blenders are easy to clean and maintain. You'll just need to prep your produce and strain your juice.

As you know by now, some nutrient-rich celery juice is better than no nutrient-rich celery juice. So a $20 blender can be a great option, especially if you're working with a tight budget. And if you do decide that you enjoy juicing and you'd like to maximize the benefits this healthy habit offers, you'll have the hands-on experience to know what you want when you upgrade. That's a win-win!

Keep the Cleanup in Mind

Blenders are infinitely easier to clean than juicers. But you'll also have to clean up your cutting board, knife, peeler, all the discards from your produce, and your strainer. Overall, that's just a few minutes' work (especially if you own a dishwasher) and may still take less time and effort than cleaning a juicer. But choosing a blender with fewer moving parts that are dishwasher safe can still help you save time and keep the cleanup to a minimum.

Pick One You Like

Just like you would with a juicer, you need to choose a blender that's going to work best for your lifestyle. Do you plan on keeping it in a cupboard? Make sure you get one that's easy to grab and lift. Or are you going to keep it on the counter? Maybe get one in a fun color that makes you happy to juice every morning. If you're intimidated by too many functions, keep it simple with a small bullet-style blender. If you love things that are high-tech, playing around with the functions on a high-performance blender might inspire you to create healthy homemade options more often. Again, make it easy on yourself so that you can make good nutrition a regular part of your life.

USING YOUR BLENDER

Any time you bring a new appliance into your home—even if it seems simple and straightforward to use—you want to read through the manufacturer's instructions. But when you drop a decent amount of money on both a blender *and* organic produce, it's even more important that you make sure you're properly maintaining the machinery! Every model has its quirks, but here are some tips and guidelines for making great juice with a blender.

Prep Your Produce

Blenders require a little more prep work than juicers. Juicing raw produce always starts with washing it thoroughly to clean off any dirt or chemical residue. But for a blender, you'll also have to remove the peel, core, pit, and seeds of your ingredients. It's especially important to remove apple seeds, which can be toxic if blended and ingested, and the membranes of citrus fruit, which can make your juice bitter.

Some professional-quality machines will make quick work of whole, hard produce. But they're the exception. More often than not, you'll need to give your produce a quick, rough chop. Check the directions for your particular blender to learn whether your ingredients need to be cut to a certain size for the machine to work well.

Keep a Safe Distance
Your blender may come with a tamper to help you push the produce down into the blades. If it doesn't, you can always use a long-handled spatula or wooden spoon. **Do not ever put your hands inside the blender.** It's all too easy to accidentally lean on a button while you adjust your produce. More often than not, you won't even need the tamper—a few quick pulses will move the produce into position.

Blend the Right Way
The first step in blending the best celery juice is to make sure you're not overloading the machine by tailoring your recipe to the blender you're using. For example, if your recipe serves four and you're using a one-serving bullet-style blender, you'll need to divide the ingredients by four. Even then, you want to be aware of how much produce your blender can handle (there's usually a fill line) and not exceed that amount, regardless of the recipe. You can always blend in batches if you need to.

Once you've added your produce to the blender, you'll need to add water to help create the right consistency. Pour in ½ cup of water for every 4 cups of produce you use. Once everything's in, make sure the lid is on tight before you start blending. (This is worth double-checking to avoid a messy disaster!)

Begin blending your juice on a medium speed (or the "chop" setting) for a few seconds, then move up to a high speed (or the "puree" setting) until the mixture is smooth. You can stop the blender and use a tamper to push any stubborn chunks down into the blades and continue blending, if necessary. Or you can try pulsing a few times in between the medium and high speeds. Just make sure you stop as soon as you get to the right consistency. Over-processing your produce can lead to the same oxidation (quick loss of nutrients and freshness) that occurs with a centrifugal juicer.

To Strain or Not to Strain
The key difference between using a juicer and using a blender to create green juice is that you'll need to strain the contents of your blender. All of the pulp that would be removed by a juicer will be mixed into your juice by a blender. This is actually a good

thing. It gives you two options: strain the blend to create your juice or don't strain it to create a fiber-filled green smoothie.

If you're using the 10-Day Celery-Powered Detox to help you get on a healthier track, you may want to wait on the smoothies. These can overload your system with fiber and cause digestive distress. Once your body gets used to having so many servings of fruit and veggies, you can introduce green smoothies for variety and even more nutrients. You'll even find ten recipes to get you started on page 161. (If you want to create truly smooth smoothies, a quality high-performance blender is your best bet, especially if you're not a fan of fibrous celery strings.)

To create your celery juice, you'll strain your blended mixture through a fine-mesh strainer or cheesecloth. To use cheesecloth, line a large container with it and slowly pour the blend into the cloth. Then gather the edges of the cloth in one hand and use your other hand to twist and squeeze the cloth to wring out the juice. To use a fine-mesh strainer or sieve, hold it over a large container with one hand while slowly pouring the blend into it with the other. The key to a mess-free transition is using a large-mouth pitcher or measuring cup—something with a spout—instead of a mixing bowl. This helps you easily pour the finished juice into a glass or to-go tumbler.

Make sure you're getting the most nutrient-rich juice out of your pulp by really wringing the cheesecloth well or pushing the pulp against the fine-mesh strainer. On the other hand, if you used a really good high-performance blender to create your juice and you're worried about excess fiber, you can strain the blend twice to make it easier on your digestive system.

Clean Your Machine

As with juicers, you need to clean your blender after every use so that bacteria don't have a chance to grow and ruin your next blend. Luckily, you only have two or three easily removed parts to wash with blenders: the cup, the blade, and the lid (though you should occasionally wipe down the base and buttons, too). Read the manufacturer's instructions so that you know whether your blender's parts can go in the dishwasher or need to be hand-washed.

Crafting Your Blends

So, you've got your brand-new juicer or blender all cleaned up and ready to use. Now comes the fun part: crafting your very own, fresh, homemade, nutrient-rich celery juice! Here are a few more things to keep in mind while you test out your new superpower. (Yes, creating your own nutritious juice is a superpower!)

KEEP IT HEALTHY

Celery-based juice may be a nutrient-dense dream of a beverage, but it can't replace well-rounded meals and it can't make up for a diet filled with junk. Always remember that you're juicing to help you become healthier and happier. That means that you're going to follow the rules of the 10-Day Celery-Powered Detox and slowly incorporate your new juicing habit into a healthy, balanced diet.

With that in mind, it's important to avoid excess sugar by maintaining the right ratio in your blends. Try to use at least three vegetables for every fruit. Fruits, fruit juice, and natural sweeteners should only be used in small amounts to brighten up the earthy flavor of your veggie blend. The celery, other veggies, and greens should be the stars of the show.

USE SERVINGS AS SUGGESTIONS

Although most recipes will list the number of servings they create, the yield actually depends a lot on several variables, such as the brand of juicer and the size and quality of the produce itself. Don't be alarmed if your yield is much more or less than the listed number of servings. You can always add ingredients if you need more juice or store any excess juice for your next drink.

DON'T STOCKPILE JUICE

Fresh is always best when it comes to the nutrients in your juice. While it may be tempting to spend Sunday blending up a week's worth of juice, you would be wasting your effort. By Thursday, your juice would be discolored, almost devoid of nutrients, and not nearly as tasty as it was on Monday. If you're using a blender or centrifugal juicer, try to drink your juice immediately. If you're using a masticating juicer, you can refrigerate your juice for up to 48 hours in an airtight container.

MIX AND MATCH YOUR PRODUCE

Celery's incredible health benefits aren't unique—many of the fruits and veggies you enjoy have equally amazing properties. Juicing celery with other organic vegetables, plus fruits and herbs, can boost its benefits and give you the variety you crave in your diet. And creating the right juice combinations ensures balanced flavors that keep you coming back for more—a must when making healthy changes!

Make sure you rotate your ingredients so that you get the full slate of nutrients available. And don't overdo it on any one addition. Not only will you get bored with using the same ingredients over and over, but you could also do more harm than good. (Certain properties in produce that are well tolerated in small amounts can become health problems in large quantities.) If you're looking to create balance in your health, you need to create balance in your juice blends! Listed here are some of the best ingredients to combine with celery.

Apples
In addition to lending a bright sweetness to your celery juice, antioxidant-rich apples can help protect heart health, bone health, and brain function. Apples can also lower your risk of stroke, ease digestion, boost your immunity, and reduce harmful inflammation thanks to their prebiotic properties and the flavonol quercetin. And if that's not enough, the polyphenols in apples have been shown to encourage weight loss and help regulate blood sugar. Just remember to remove the stem, core, and seeds from your apples before adding them to your juice.

Beets
Beets lend celery juice their deep red color while helping to protect your heart and brain health—their nitrates increase oxygen flow, helping to lower blood pressure and improve cognitive function. Studies show they even reduce the risk of dementia. And thanks to the betalains in beets, eating and juicing them can help reduce inflammation and improve kidney function. When combined with celery juice, beets are a great way to support your body's natural digestive and detox functions. Just keep in mind that, if you want your blends to taste a little less earthy, you can always peel beets before juicing them. Choose beets that are heavy with perky green, leafy tops.

Blueberries
Blueberries are considered a superfood thanks to their high levels of free-radical-fighting antioxidants. In addition to reducing oxidative cell damage, they can help lower blood pressure, prevent heart disease, improve brain function, and reduce insulin sensitivity in people with type 2 diabetes. That means that blueberries are a safe addition for those watching their blood sugar (in moderation, of course). You can find blueberries year-round, but if you're lucky enough to have an organic farm near you, picking your own is the most nutritious option.

Carrots
You may already know that the carotenoids in carrots are wonderful for your eye health, but did you know that those same carotene antioxidants have also been linked to a reduced risk of developing certain types of cancer? Plus, carrots can help lower your cholesterol, maintain your weight, and balance your blood sugar. To ensure the most nutrients, buy vibrantly colored whole carrots rather than baby carrots. You can even add the leafy tops of the carrots to your blend for an extra dose of vitamins and minerals. But just like its relative celery, carrots can cause an allergic reaction. If you're sensitive to birch or mugwort pollen, you may have a carrot allergy.

Cilantro
Cilantro offers the same carotenoids as carrots, which means it, too, can help protect your vision and reduce the risk of certain cancers. It also aids digestion by helping your body produce digestive enzymes that break down food. And thanks to its antimicrobial and detoxifying properties, cilantro is being studied as a natural water purifier. Not bad for a little herb! Look for fresh bunches of cilantro with full, fragrant, bright green leaves.

rs

are cucumbers a crisp and refreshing addition to celery juice, but they're also
ith antioxidants for fending off chronic illnesses. Their pectin and high water
pport healthy digestion as well as weight loss and help maintain blood sugar
cumbers keep a good amount of their nutrients in their peel, so make sure you
whole and unpeeled to your meal plan in addition to juicing them. The best
rs are firm, dark green, and without blemishes or soft spots. Make sure you buy
nes because cucumbers are also a member of the EWG's Dirty Dozen.

Fennel adds to the spice of celery juice with a mild licorice flavor. With 17 percent of your
recommended Daily Value of antioxidant vitamin C in 1 cup, fennel can also help you
fend off everything from the common cold to chronic illness. Like celery, fennel gives your
bone health a boost as a good source of potassium, magnesium, and manganese. When
shopping for it, look for large white or green bulbs without splitting. The fronds shouldn't
have flowers and the bottom should be free of brown spots. When juice recipes call for
fennel, they tend to mean the bulb, but you can also juice the stalks and leaves.

Ginger
Ginger is not only a great flavor to combine with celery, but it's also chock-full of nutritional benefits. This little root is packed with gingerol, a bioactive compound with powerful antioxidant and anti-inflammatory properties. In addition, it can help treat nausea and
morning sickness, soothe indigestion, reduce muscle pain and soreness from exercise,
ease arthritis pain, lower blood sugar and cholesterol, and protect against heart disease.
And if that's not enough, it also inhibits the growth of bacteria and fights gum disease.
Look for fresh ginger that has thin, shiny skin and a strong, spicy smell but no soft spots.

Kale
Another superfood, kale is one of the most nutrient-dense ingredients you can find. To
give you an example, it packs in 206 percent of your recommend Daily Value of vitamin
A, 134 percent of vitamin C, and 684 percent of vitamin K. That means it's loaded with
antioxidants that have anti-inflammatory, antiviral, antidepressant, and anticancer effects.
Kale can also help your blood clot, prevent osteoporosis, give you more energy, reduce
your risk of diabetes, and protect your heart health. But before you start adding it to
everything you eat, you'll need to know that kale is also a goitrogenic food. Consuming
too much of it can lead to enlarged thyroid glands. Aim for about 5 cups of crisp, dark
green, small-leaved organic kale per week.

Tomatoes

If you're looking forward to making a nutrient-rich version of vegetable juice at home, you'll need to start with some nutrient-rich tomatoes. With their vitamin C, lycopene, chlorogenic acid, and beta-carotene, tomatoes can help reduce your risk of heart disease and stroke. And, of course, they're full of free radical–fighting antioxidants, which can help reduce your risk of cancer and chronic illness. Tomatoes are easy to grow at home, but if you're at the store, look for large tomatoes with a deep, consistent color that feel heavy for their size. The best ones have a strong, slightly sweet, earthy smell.

Wheatgrass

Wheatgrass is a staple of commercial juice bars, and for good reason. Not only does it add a light, green tea–like flavor to your celery juice, but it also adds even more vitamins and antioxidants. Wheatgrass can help lower cholesterol, regulate blood sugar, reduce inflammation, and support weight loss. Some studies show that wheatgrass could even help kill certain types of cancer cells. Unfortunately, wheatgrass is especially susceptible to mold, which can cause it to taste bitter. For the best flavor, look for fresh, organic wheatgrass that was grown outside (rather than in a greenhouse). You can also grow your own!

DON'T WASTE THE PULP

You might be wondering what to do with all the pulp that comes from juicing so many fruits and veggies. One great option is to compost it. But you can also use it to create veggie broth for soups, add it to veggie burgers, and turn it into snacks such as energy balls, fruit leather, and baked goods. A quick online search can turn up dozens of ways to make the most of *all* of your produce's nutrients.

Are You Ready?

If you're excited to get healthy and feel amazing, you're going to love what comes next. You'll take the knowledge you've gained about what fresh, nutrient-rich produce can do for your body and use it to change your life. The 10-Day Celery-Powered Detox will set you up for long-term success by teaching you how to incorporate juicing into a wellness plan that works for *you*. You're just ten days away from a healthier, happier you. Are you ready? Turn the page!

PART 3

The 10-Day Celery-Powered Detox

Now that you know all about the incredible nutritional benefits packed into each stalk of celery, you're ready to make some celery juice! In fact, you're ready to tackle this whole healthy eating thing and start feeling better than you ever have. Well, good news! The ten-day detox plan you're about to discover is the road map you need to start your wellness journey off right.

This isn't your ordinary detox, with promises that you'll shed pounds quickly only to gain them back just as fast. Sure, the 10-Day Celery-Powered Detox can help you lose weight. But the real miracle of celery juice is what it can help you gain—a long, happy, healthy life. Combined with the right foods and habits, celery juice can help your body find its perfect balance.

With that in mind, this ten-day detox doesn't involve starving yourself—a decidedly unhealthy habit. And it doesn't force you to drink large quantities of celery juice alone, which can cause some very unpleasant side effects. During these first ten days of your journey, you'll drink two small glasses of homemade juice a day, accompanied by protein-rich snacks and nutritious meals. This gives your body time to adjust (resulting in fewer unwanted side effects) and sets you up for long-term success.

The 10-Day Celery-Powered Detox is simple, straightforward, and focused on putting your well-being first. But you're ready for more than just a diet plan. You're ready to take back your health and maximize the benefits you get from your detox. That means customizing the plan to your health needs, rounding out your wellness routine, and getting in the right headspace for success. Once you get to know your detox plan, keep reading for more tips on how to do exactly that.

Your 10-Day Detox Plan

The 10-Day Celery-Powered Detox is no one-size-fits-all cleanse. Instead, it gives you a customizable framework to become your healthiest self. What your plan looks like is entirely up to you, because only you (and your health care professional) know what you need and what you like. And liking your plan is important! Not only will you stick with it longer, but you'll also feel amazing.

WHAT'S INCLUDED

You don't need to trick your body into detoxing, which is something it already does on a regular basis. You're just the coach. You need to support your team (your immune, kidney, liver, and gastrointestinal systems) with proper nutrition and a positive mind-set.

The specifics are up to you, but for best results, every day of your detox should include the following:

- **Homemade celery-based juice.** You'll drink two small (8- to 12-ounce) glasses of juice per day, one in the morning and one in the afternoon, to help flush out any toxins.
- **Protein-rich snacks.** Protein is one thing you can't get from fruits and vegetables, and it's an incredibly important building block for a healthy body. It's also a macronutrient, meaning your body needs a lot of it. Plus, including protein in all of your snacks and meals will keep you feeling full and happy in between them.
- **Complete and balanced meals.** Well-rounded meals are another way to support all the hard work your celery juice is doing to revitalize your body. Yours should include a variety of healthy proteins, fats, and carbohydrates (think salmon and quinoa, not bacon cheese fries), as well as whole fruits and vegetables, which should account for half of your plate.
- **Eight glasses of water.** Celery juice is a great source of hydration, but adding eight glasses of water to your day can help clear out even more toxins and keep all of your body's processes running smoothly.
- **Some sort of exercise.** Celery is pretty amazing, but it can't exercise for you. Whether you do an hour of CrossFit, attend a yoga class, or go for a walk, make sure you're moving your body for at least 30 minutes every day to support good digestion.

MAKE WAY FOR MAGIC

Making sure you're eating the right stuff is only a part of the equation. You also have to clear the way for celery juice to work its magic during your detox. That means creating less work for your body's natural detoxification process by eliminating certain foods from your diet (or at least limiting them) so that your body doesn't have to. These include:

- **Alcohol.** A glass of wine may have all the health benefits of those grapes in your green juice, but the fermentation and dehydration aren't great for your system. Instead of making your liver do the extra work, just purge alcohol from your diet for these ten days and let celery juice do its thing. Then you're welcome to work the wine back in.
- **Coffee.** This one can be tricky for some people, but coffee can actually interfere with your liver's detoxification processes. If you can't give it up entirely, at least try to cut back to one cup a day. Studies show that you should wait until

between 10 a.m. and 12 p.m. for that one cup to receive the most effective energy boost. After a couple of days of energizing green juice, you won't even miss it!

- **Milk and milk products.** Did you know that you might be lactose intolerant? A lot of adults are. Milk could be upsetting your digestion, which would make it harder for celery juice to help your body detox. Try going without it for a few days and you'll feel the difference! If you do incorporate dairy, make it light and high in protein—low-fat cottage cheese or unsweetened Greek yogurt, for example.

- **Red meat.** Red meat can make your digestive system move in slow motion and throw a wrench in your detox. Steer clear of it during your ten-day detox and your stomach will thank you. Challenge yourself to find delicious veggie, chicken, and fish alternatives.

- **Refined sugar.** How would you like to lose weight, get clearer skin, and boost your heart health with one move? Just skip the added sugar whenever possible and your dreams can come true! The good news is that studies show that drinking celery juice can reduce sugar cravings. So once you've finished your ten-day detox, you may find a low-sugar diet pretty easy to keep up with.

- **Soda (and other carbonated beverages).** The sugar content alone makes eliminating regular soda a no-brainer. But if a flatter stomach is part of the reason that you're excited to try the 10-Day Celery-Powered detox, then you'll want to avoid all carbonated beverages because they cause gas and bloating. That includes seltzer water and sugar-free sodas. Luckily, yummy celery juice blends can fill that soda-shaped hole in your day.

The 10-Day Celery-Powered Detox Plan

If you're sick and tired of feeling sick and tired, get ready to transform your health! Just ten days can make all the difference—especially when celery juice is involved.

You'll notice that the 10-Day Celery-Powered Detox suggests two servings of juice per day, but some recipes in this book create one serving. That's meant to maximize the nutrients in the juice. If you don't want to haul out and clean the juicer twice, go ahead and double the recipe so that it makes two servings. Regardless of which appliance you use, a few hours in the fridge won't make a huge difference. And the point of the plan is to create a juicing habit that works for you. If you occasionally need to sacrifice a few nutrients in order to enjoy two glasses of celery-based juice a day, that's OK!

DAY 1

Breakfast
Drink one 8- to 12-ounce glass of detox-approved juice with a healthy side.
Example: Unsweetened peanut butter on whole-grain toast.

AM Snack
Eat a healthy snack of your choice.
Example: Veggies (such as celery) and hummus.

Lunch
Eat a healthy lunch of your choice.
Example: Spinach salad topped with grilled chicken.

PM Snack
Drink a second 8- to 12-ounce glass of detox-approved juice.

Dinner
Eat a healthy dinner of your choice.
Example: Grilled salmon with quinoa and steamed broccoli.

Daily Habits
Drink at least 8 glasses of water and get at least 30 minutes of exercise.

Today's Recommended Detox Recipe

Fresh Start
Servings: 1
2 medium stalks celery
1 large apple, cored and seeded
3 medium carrots
1 (½-inch) piece ginger, peeled
¾ cup water
Juice of ½ medium lemon or lime

Juicer: Follow the instructions for your particular appliance, stirring the water and lemon or lime juice into the finished mixture. Refrigerate any unused juice in an airtight container for up to 48 hours.

Blender: Peel and roughly chop all the produce before blending it together, then strain the mixture. Stir the water and lemon or lime juice into the finished juice. Refrigerate any unused juice in an airtight container for up to 48 hours.

DAY 2

Breakfast
Drink one 8- to 12-ounce glass of detox-approved juice with a healthy side.
Example: A handful of almonds.

AM Snack
Eat a healthy snack of your choice.
Example: Celery with unsweetened peanut butter.

Lunch
Eat a healthy lunch of your choice.
Example: Minestrone soup.

PM Snack
Drink a second 8- to 12-ounce glass of detox-approved juice.

Dinner
Eat a healthy dinner of your choice.
Example: Sheet-pan chicken breast with roasted vegetables.

Daily Habits
Drink at least 8 glasses of water and get at least 30 minutes of exercise.

Today's Recommended Detox Recipe

Easy Does It
Servings: 1
4 medium stalks celery
2 medium apples, cored and seeded
3 medium carrots

Juicer: Follow the instructions for your particular appliance. Refrigerate any unused juice in an airtight container for up to 48 hours.

Blender: Peel and roughly chop all the produce before blending it together, then strain the mixture. Refrigerate any unused juice in an airtight container for up to 48 hours.

DAY 3

Breakfast
Drink one 8- to 12-ounce glass of detox-approved juice with a healthy side.
Example: A hard-boiled egg.

AM Snack
Eat a healthy snack of your choice.
Example: Red bell pepper with homemade guacamole.

Lunch
Eat a healthy lunch of your choice.
Example: Hearty salad with avocado and black beans.

PM Snack
Drink a second 8- to 12-ounce glass of detox-approved juice.

Dinner
Eat a healthy dinner of your choice.
Example: Zucchini noodles in a lemon-herb sauce with chicken.

Daily Habits
Drink at least 8 glasses of water and get at least 30 minutes of exercise.

Today's Recommended Detox Recipe

All the Bases
Servings: 1
3 medium stalks celery

(Continued on page 51)

1 small red beet
2 medium carrots
½ medium lemon, peeled
1 medium green apple, cored and seeded
1 (1-inch) piece ginger, peeled

Juicer: Follow the instructions for your particular appliance. Refrigerate any unused juice in an airtight container for up to 48 hours.

Blender: Peel and roughly chop all the produce before blending it together, then strain the mixture. Refrigerate any unused juice in an airtight container for up to 48 hours.

DAY 4

Breakfast
Drink one 8- to 12-ounce glass of detox-approved juice with a healthy side.
Example: Avocado on whole-grain toast.

AM Snack
Eat a healthy snack of your choice.
Example: Celery with low-fat cream cheese and pineapple.

Lunch
Eat a healthy lunch of your choice.
Example: Lettuce wraps with tuna.

PM Snack
Drink a second 8- to 12-ounce glass of detox-approved juice.

Dinner
Eat a healthy dinner of your choice.
Example: Grilled chicken and veggie kabobs.

Daily Habits
Drink at least 8 glasses of water and get at least 30 minutes of exercise.

Today's Recommended Detox Recipe

Super Green
Servings: 1
2 medium stalks celery, without leaves
1 medium green apple, cored and seeded
½ small cucumber
1 small handful kale
½ medium lemon, peeled
1 (½-inch) piece ginger, peeled

Juicer: Follow the instructions for your particular appliance. Refrigerate any unused juice in an airtight container for up to 48 hours.

Blender: Peel and roughly chop all the produce before blending it together, then strain the mixture. Refrigerate any unused juice in an airtight container for up to 48 hours.

DAY 5

Breakfast
Drink one 8- to 12-ounce glass of detox-approved juice with a healthy side.
Example: A handful of pistachios.

AM Snack
Eat a healthy snack of your choice.
Example: Apple or banana slices topped with unsweetened peanut butter.

Lunch
Eat a healthy lunch of your choice.
Example: Low-sodium chicken soup with chickpeas, kale, and mushrooms.

PM Snack
Drink a second 8- to 12-ounce glass of detox-approved juice.

Dinner
Eat a healthy dinner of your choice.
Example: Garlic-marinated shrimp with couscous.

Daily Habits
Drink at least 8 glasses of water and get at least 30 minutes of exercise.

Today's Recommended Detox Recipe

Deep Red Detox
Servings: 1
3 medium stalks celery
3 small red beets
3 small carrots
1 (1-inch) piece ginger, peeled

Juicer: Follow the instructions for your particular appliance. Refrigerate any unused juice in an airtight container for up to 48 hours.

Blender: Peel and roughly chop all the produce before blending it together, then strain the mixture. Refrigerate any unused juice in an airtight container for up to 48 hours.

DAY 6

Breakfast
Drink one 8- to 12-ounce glass of detox-approved juice with a healthy side.
Example: A handful of roasted chickpeas.

AM Snack
Eat a healthy snack of your choice.
Example: Kale chips.

Lunch
Eat a healthy lunch of your choice.
Example: Turkey rollups with spinach and tomatoes.

PM Snack
Drink a second 8- to 12-ounce glass of detox-approved juice.

Dinner
Eat a healthy dinner of your choice.
Example: Veggie omelet (without cheese).

Daily Habits
Drink at least 8 glasses of water and get at least 30 minutes of exercise.

Today's Recommended Detox Recipe

Simple but Mighty
Servings: 1
4 medium stalks celery
1 medium apple, cored and seeded
1 (¼-inch) piece ginger, peeled
¼ medium lime or lemon, peeled

Juicer: Follow the instructions for your particular appliance. Refrigerate any unused juice in an airtight container for up to 48 hours.

Blender: Peel and roughly chop all the produce before blending it together, then strain the mixture. Refrigerate any unused juice in an airtight container for up to 48 hours.

DAY 7

Breakfast
Drink one 8- to 12-ounce glass of detox-approved juice with a healthy side.
Example: A small bowl of low-sugar or unsweetened cereal (without milk).

AM Snack
Eat a healthy snack of your choice.
Example: Pear slices with light ricotta cheese.

Lunch
Eat a healthy lunch of your choice.
Example: Hearty salad topped with chickpeas and vegetables.

PM Snack
Drink a second 8- to 12-ounce glass of detox-approved juice.

But if you're only drinking celery juice, you're not maximizing its benefits. Mixing and matching your ingredients is not only great for the flavor of your juice, but it's also going to turn your juice into a powerful multivitamin. Check out "Mix and Match Your Produce" on page 34 for some of the best ingredients to combine with celery and their incredible health benefits.

HYDRATION

Put simply: the more water your drink, the better you'll look and feel. Staying properly hydrated helps your digestive system run smoothly, which means your celery juice can get right to work. Your skin will be clearer, your stomach will feel better, and you'll have more energy. Plus, drinking plenty of water will also help you feel fuller and keep hunger at bay while you adjust to your new routine. When your stomach rumbles, it could just be letting you know that it needs some hydration. Give it a glass of water before turning to a healthy snack.

EXERCISE

If you're looking to boost your overall health, you need to think beyond your diet. Regular exercise can help celery juice work its magic on your energy levels, digestion, heart health, and more. Don't worry! That doesn't mean you have to start running marathons. Studies show that a 30-minute walk (or even three 10-minute walks) will do the trick. The point is to get your body moving *in some way* to help kick-start your metabolism and help the nutrients in your celery juice get to where they need to go. A daily walk alone has been shown to boost your mood, improve your body's response to insulin, prevent muscle loss, improve digestion, and lower your risk of chronic disease. Now combine that with the nutritional benefits of celery juice, and just imagine how great you're going to feel!

Tips for Success

The 10-Day Celery-Powered Detox is just the beginning of a lifetime of celery juice helping you look and feel great, so you'll want to use it to create a strong foundation you can build on. Set yourself up for success right from the start and you'll have no problem making those healthy habits stick. If you really want to make the most of the benefits of celery juice, keep these tips and tricks in mind.

GIVE YOURSELF A LITTLE TASTE

Before you start your detox, try adding a small glass of celery-based juice to your routine just a couple of times a week without changing anything else. If you're new to juicing, this gives you a chance to get familiar with the process and learn what you like in a juice. It also lets your body know it's time to gear up for healthier things to come.

GO SLOWLY

With all of celery juice's amazing benefits, you might be tempted to sneak a little more into each day. But these first ten days are about feeling good and getting your body used to your new routine. Drinking lots of celery juice can speed the detox process, but it won't feel good! Each of the recipes in this book offers a potential number of servings, but actual results can vary depending on your juicer, your process, and your produce. If a recipe makes more than 8 to 12 ounces of juice, save the excess juice for later by storing it in an airtight container in the refrigerator.

START WITH AN EMPTY STOMACH

This one won't be hard to do, because you'll wake up looking forward to that refreshing glass of celery juice. Drinking your juice first thing in the morning on an empty stomach means that nothing can come between those nutrients and your body. You'll absorb the nutrients faster and feel great sooner. Follow the juice up with a protein-rich snack, which will gather up any straggling nutrients and help your body absorb them, too.

MAXIMIZE YOUR DETOX

Want to know what celery juice can do for you? Stick to detox-specific recipes for the first ten days. When you're following the detox plan, you don't have to use a particular day's detox recipe, but you should stick to the recipes contained within the ten-day plan. These have been specifically tailored to get the most detox power out of your celery juice. When you finish the detox, you can explore all of the delicious juice recipes starting on page 69 to maximize your health benefits. Plus, you can start creating your own wonderful, nutrient-rich blends based on what you've learned during your detox.

MAKE THE RECIPES WORK FOR YOU

The 10-Day Celery-Powered Detox is all about making healthy work for *you*. While you should stick to the detox recipes as closely as possible to get all of their incredible benefits, don't feel guilty about substituting something you like for something you don't. Just try to make similar substitutions (green veggie for green veggie, citrus fruit for citrus fruit). If you're one of the large percentage of people who can't stand cilantro, skip it altogether! Check out "Mix and Match Your Produce" on page 34 for some ideas of how to get the same benefits from different fruits and veggies. You have to make the plan work for you, or it won't work at all.

EAT!

Don't be alarmed if your stomach starts to rumble more often than it used to. You may be used to eating more calories than you think, which means your stomach will start loudly protesting your new routine. If you *think* you're hungry, then have a glass of water. If you *know* you're hungry, then eat! Just be mindful and keep it healthy. You can even use it as an opportunity to incorporate more celery into your diet: top a stalk with unsweetened peanut butter, hummus, or cream cheese and pineapple for a snack that's as filling and nutritious as it is tasty.

GIVE YOURSELF A BREAK

One of the most important things you can do to ensure your detox success is to remember that you're human. As you go through the detox, you may give in to that chocolate craving one night or decide you really need a little piece of steak. That's OK! Developing healthy habits isn't like flipping a switch. Focus on feeling healthy and happy rather than being perfect, and you'll be able to get yourself right back on track when you slip.

GET PLENTY OF SLEEP

In case you needed another excuse to hit snooze in the morning, sleep is just as important for your detox as it is for your good mood! When you're sleep-deprived, toxins can build up in your system. Over time, that can lead to anxiety, high blood pressure, heart disease, obesity, and even Alzheimer's. Juicing can't make up for sleep deprivation, so it's important to take sleep seriously. Getting 7 to 9 hours of quality sleep per night can help your body get rid of built-up toxins so that the nutrients in your morning celery juice can get right to work. If you have a hard time getting to sleep, try establishing a set schedule that includes staying away from screens of any kind right before bed (that includes television, computer, *and* phone).

STAY POSITIVE AND ENJOY THE JOURNEY

The only way to meet a goal is to have one in mind. What do you hope to get out of your detox? Changing up your diet and your routine isn't easy. Get clear on what you want, and then have faith that you'll get there. Remind yourself often of how incredible you'll feel when you clear out the junk food and rebalance your body. When you go for your daily walk, really take the time to notice and enjoy the things around you. And most of all, congratulate yourself on the small wins—creating a great juice, eating a nutritious meal, getting some exercise. Staying relaxed and positive throughout the detox period will have a big impact on your success. And if you experience a setback, don't beat yourself up. Just keep moving forward.

KNOW THAT YOU HAVE EVERYTHING YOU NEED

The 10-Day Celery-Powered Detox has everything you need to revitalize your body and feel great. That means you don't need any of those other products on the market that promise to help detoxify your body, many of which use strong diuretics and laxatives. Instead, you'll gently support your body's natural detoxification process for great results without the unpleasant effects of harsh products.

What to Expect When You're Detoxing

During your 10-Day Celery-Powered Detox, you're going to be making healthy changes left and right. From boosting your nutrient intake to moving your body, those changes are going to make you look and feel amazing. Keep it up, and they'll help protect your heart, improve your brain function, strengthen your bones, and fend off chronic illness! But whenever you make a change to your diet, you should expect to experience a few growing pains. If you do notice any issues, just deal with them as they come.

BATHROOM BREAKS

Celery juice doesn't just help you maximize the nutrients you need to stay healthy. It also helps you flush out the toxins that could make you feel sluggish or sick by acting as a natural diuretic and laxative. That's what makes it so perfect for a ten-day detox! But that means that you'll need to make more frequent trips to the bathroom. For your convenience, make sure that you have ready access to one during your detox.

CAFFEINE WITHDRAWAL

If you've given up coffee as part of your detox, you could experience caffeine withdrawal. Symptoms are going to depend on how much caffeine you're used to drinking in a day, but you can expect some headaches and grouchiness while you adjust. That's nothing that an over-the-counter pain med (and maybe a nap) can't handle! But between your celery juice—which is full of energizing B vitamins and water—and your daily exercise, you might find that you feel even better without that morning cup of joe.

CRAVINGS

When you're used to indulging in less-than-healthy options, it's almost impossible to stop cold turkey. And there's no need to! Instead, just keep that moderation mind-set. If you can't get over a craving, give yourself a little bit of whatever it is that you want. You'll find that you don't need a whole candy bar to satisfy a chocolate craving, for example—a bite will do. But the best thing to do is grab a healthy, protein-rich alternative with some natural sweetness: a few strawberries dipped in low-fat cottage cheese, for example. Within a couple of days of celery juice working its magic, those cravings might start to disappear entirely.

LOW ENERGY

Flushing out toxins is hard work, so you might find your energy naturally dipping from time to time during your detox. If you're a big fan of afternoon naps, take advantage of this by having a snooze in the sunshine to recharge. If you're someone who feels guilty taking breaks, this is your justification to give yourself some much-needed "me time." While your body adjusts to its new routine, don't feel guilty about resting when you need to. But don't use fatigue as an excuse to skip your daily exercise, either. A 30-minute walk might actually be just what you need to shake that tired feeling.

IRRITABILITY

If you're used to indulging in junk foods, you may be a little cranky during your detox. And you know what? You're allowed to be—at first. But within a couple of days, that celery juice will start to light you up from the inside and make you realize how wonderful you're going to feel on Day 10. Whenever you're missing your usual indulgences, treat yourself to an alternative pick-me-up. Your daily walk could do the trick, or maybe a favorite TV show. Indulge in experiences that make you happy and you won't miss the junk food.

SKIN ISSUES

Ditching added sugar, dairy, and red meat in favor of celery juice is a sure-fire way to get clearer, healthier skin. But as you go through your detox, you may notice some pimples popping up. Don't fret! Your skin may go through a purge phase, where it's moving toxins up and out through your pores. This is a good thing! It means the detox is working. Just make sure you're cleansing and moisturizing regularly to help the celery juice do its job. Your body will reward your patience with a glowing complexion.

BE AWARE OF GOITROGENS

As you've probably realized by now, too much of any good thing can sometimes be a bad thing. If you're someone who has experience with goiters (enlarged thyroid glands), know that consuming large amounts of certain raw fruits and vegetables can cause them. Goitrogens, as they're called, include broccoli, cabbage, cauliflower, celery, kale, peaches, spinach, and strawberries. When you're mixing your blends, be aware of how many of these ingredients make it in.

WATCH YOUR SUGAR

Any juice that you make should heavily favor vegetables due to the high sugar content in many fruits, but this is especially true if you're watching your blood sugar. People with diabetes should steer clear of high-glycemic fruits entirely. These include banana, grapes, kiwi, mango, melons, papaya, and pineapple. Instead, stick with apples, berries, cherries, and citrus fruits, and always add them to your daily diet in moderation. If blood sugar is a concern for you, make sure you talk to a health care professional before beginning the plan and monitor your blood sugar throughout, making adjustments when necessary.

BALANCE YOUR SODIUM

You may have heard that celery is comparatively high in sodium, but celery is not what your doctor would consider a "high-sodium food." One stalk contains approximately 35 milligrams of sodium. Compare that with the American Heart Association's recommended daily maximum of 1,500 milligrams per day and you realize that one or two stalks a day is a drop in the bucket. So, even if you're watching your sodium, you can feel good about adding heart-healthy celery to your juice blends. Just be mindful of your sodium intake and careful not to overdo it on higher-sodium vegetables such as beets, carrots, Swiss chard, and spinach. Add them to blends with plenty of lower-sodium vegetables and fruits to balance them out.

You've Got This!

Congratulations! You've completed the 10-Day Celery-Powered Detox, and you should be really proud of yourself. Keep the momentum going by maintaining your newly balanced diet and wellness routine. You can slowly begin to add back in some of the foods and beverages you've excluded, but make sure you don't undo all of your hard work. You feel amazing, and you want to keep it that way!

Now that you've gotten used to juicing, you're ready to experiment with new and scrumptious recipes. Starting on the next page, you'll find fifty of them to help you feel your best. And because you've let your body get used to its new routine, you can start to shake things up. Mix up a 16-ounce blend for breakfast on the go, have a tall glass in the afternoon as a pick-me-up, or just stick with the small servings and use them as snacks between meals. The point is to create a juicing habit that works for you. Don't be afraid to take your time figuring out what that looks like. It will be a deliciously healthy journey!

PART 4

Juice and Smoothie Recipes

Juice Recipes for Your Health

Hopefully by now, you've come to realize that adding celery to your diet comes with some amazing health benefits. You've also learned that celery isn't the only powerhouse in the produce section: nutritional benefits, like flavors, abound. You'll find endless ways to mix and match fruits, vegetables, herbs, and roots to create juice recipes that your taste buds will love as much as your body will.

Learning to create a juice recipe is a process. What you put into your body is entirely up to you; it depends on your personal preferences, your health needs, and the produce you're able to find locally. Once you learn what you like in a juice recipe and which ingredients offer the nutrients you need, you can begin to create your own blends. But the only way to know what works well for you is to try as many recipes as possible.

That's why you'll find fifty recipes in the following pages to start you off. These blends are organized by their greatest benefits, such as increased energy or digestive support. But don't let that keep you from trying recipes in all of the categories—every one of these blends is chock-full of nutrients that can help make you a happier, healthier human.

Just keep in mind that moderation and variety are key. While it's wonderful to find a juice that you can't get enough of, your body needs an assortment of nutrients. Too much of any one ingredient or blend can start to cause side effects. (For example, the right amount of fiber can relieve bloating while too much fiber can cause it.) Keep searching and creating until you find several recipes you love that you can incorporate into your wellness routine.

If you need a refresher on the juicing process, turn to page 22. Here are a few more quick tips to keep in mind when making any of these recipes:

- **Be sure to use the highest-quality organic produce whenever possible.** And make sure you wash your ingredients well. Remember, you won't be cooking anything, so it's important that your ingredients be clean and pesticide-free.
- **To get the most benefit, drink your juice while it's fresh.** You can also store it, covered, for up to two days in the refrigerator. If you want to prep blends ahead of time, you can freeze them without losing any nutrients. (Try creating your own juice ice pops for a refreshing treat on a warm day!)
- **Once you've tried a recipe as it's written, don't be afraid to experiment.** You can swap out ingredients you're not crazy about, lower or increase written amounts,

and add things you think will benefit the blend. Soon enough, you'll find your perfect flavor balance.

There's no better time than the present to start reaping the health benefits of celery-based juice blends. So, dive in and enjoy!

AGING

Coconut Refresher Blend

If you're looking for antiaging benefits but you're not a fan of deep-green juice, this refreshing blend might be perfect for you. Coconut water and apples keep things light while offering up plenty of hydration for thirsty skin. Add in the antioxidant benefits of celery and blueberries and you get a blend that feels as refreshing as it tastes.

Servings: 2

Ingredients:
2 medium stalks celery
2 cups blueberries
2 medium red apples, cored and seeded
1 cup coconut water

Juicer: Follow the instructions for your particular appliance, stirring the coconut water into the finished mixture. Refrigerate any unused juice in an airtight container for up to 48 hours.

Blender: Peel and roughly chop all the produce before blending it together, then strain the mixture. Stir the coconut water into the strained juice. Refrigerate any unused juice in an airtight container for up to 48 hours.

Antioxidant Youth Tonic

The powerful mix of vitamins and antioxidants in this juice fights the signs of aging from the inside and out by protecting your heart, bones, eyes, and cognitive function as well as nourishing your skin and hair. Drink this blend regularly to restore your youthful glow and vitality.

Servings: 2

Ingredients:
2 medium stalks celery
1 small red beet
2 large carrots
1 handful kale
1 medium green apple, cored and seeded
Juice of ½ medium lime

Juicer: Follow the instructions for your particular appliance, stirring the lime juice into the finished mixture. Refrigerate any unused juice in an airtight container for up to 48 hours.

Blender: Peel and roughly chop all the produce before blending it together, then strain the mixture. Stir the lime juice into the finished juice. Refrigerate any unused juice in an airtight container for up to 48 hours.

Carrot-Infused Sun Care

Wearing sunscreen every time you step outside is crucial to keeping your skin healthy and youthful. But consuming the beta-carotene found in vegetables like carrots and kale can also help protect your skin from the damaging effects of the sun, including common skin cancers. While this is a great juice to add to your regular routine, it could prove especially useful in the summer, when you're spending more time outdoors.

Servings: 1

Ingredients:
2 medium stalks celery
1 handful kale
1 medium apple, cored and seeded
½ medium lemon, peeled
6 large carrots

Juicer: Follow the instructions for your particular appliance. Refrigerate any unused juice in an airtight container for up to 48 hours.

Blender: Peel and roughly chop all the produce before blending it together, then strain the mixture. Refrigerate any unused juice in an airtight container for up to 48 hours.

ALLERGIES

All-Natural Antihistamine

Allergens cause cells in the body to produce histamines, which result in those annoying allergy symptoms you experience, such as itchy, watery eyes. The vitamin C in fruits like pineapple and lemon can help prevent the formation of histamines while the quercetin in apples can help inhibit them. Together, they make a mighty anti-allergy concoction.

Servings: 2

Ingredients:
4 medium stalks celery
½ cup chopped parsley
1 medium cucumber
1 medium apple, cored and seeded
1 medium lemon, peeled
1 cup chopped pineapple

Juicer: Follow the instructions for your particular appliance. Refrigerate any unused juice in an airtight container for up to 48 hours.

Blender: Peel and roughly chop all the produce before blending it together, then strain the mixture. Refrigerate any unused juice in an airtight container for up to 48 hours.

Honey-Lemon Hay Fever Relief

If allergy season makes you want to stay in bed, try adding this parsley-rich blend to your daily routine. One of celery's close relatives, parsley is a well-known natural allergy remedy that offers detoxifying and anti-inflammatory properties. Adding cucumber, lemon, and apples to the mix tempers parsley's tendency toward bitterness, and a bit of local honey helps ward off regional allergens.

Servings: 2

Ingredients:
2 medium stalks celery
1 bunch flat-leaf parsley
1 medium cucumber
2 medium lemons, peeled
1 medium green apple, cored and seeded
1 (1-inch) piece ginger, peeled
1 teaspoon locally harvested honey

Juicer: Follow the instructions for your particular appliance, stirring the honey into the finished mixture. Refrigerate any unused juice in an airtight container for up to 48 hours.

Blender: Peel and roughly chop all the produce before blending it together, then strain the mixture. Stir the honey into the finished juice. Refrigerate any unused juice in an airtight container for up to 48 hours.

Ginger-Cayenne Sinus Rescue

Allergy symptoms are all irritating, but sinus congestion may be the worst of all. That stuffy, uncomfortable feeling gives way to a throbbing headache and takes away your ability to focus. That's when you reach for this recipe. Ginger and a hint of cayenne pepper clear your sinuses while a heaping helping of vitamin C keeps your body from producing the histamines that are making you so miserable.

Servings: 1

Ingredients:
2 large stalks celery
1 (2-inch-thick) slice pineapple
2 medium oranges, peeled
1 medium lemon, peeled
1 (1-inch) piece ginger, peeled
1 pinch cayenne pepper

Juicer: Follow the instructions for your particular appliance, stirring the cayenne pepper into the finished mixture. Refrigerate any unused juice in an airtight container for up to 48 hours.

Blender: Peel and roughly chop all the produce before blending it together, then strain the mixture. Stir the cayenne pepper into the finished juice. Refrigerate any unused juice in an airtight container for up to 48 hours.

BEAUTY

Green Glow

Sometimes the simplest skin care is the most effective, which is why this green juice keeps the ingredient list short. This blend has everything you need to hydrate and nourish your skin for a glowing complexion. While the apples should balance out the bitterness of the kale, you can also add a splash of lemon juice for flavor and an extra shot of skin-loving antioxidants.

Servings: 3

Ingredients:
6 large stalks celery
1 handful kale
4 large apples. cored and seeded

Juicer: Follow the instructions for your particular appliance. Refrigerate any unused juice in an airtight container for up to 48 hours.

Blender: Peel and roughly chop all the produce before blending it together, then strain the mixture. Refrigerate any unused juice in an airtight container for up to 48 hours.

Spinach Skin Detox

Our skin is often a reflection of how we treat our bodies. If you've been burning the midnight oil, not getting enough sleep, and grabbing junk food on the go, this blend can help you get back on the right track. Parsley detoxifies, spinach provides essential fatty acids to protect your skin, and carrots have beta-carotene to combat inflammation and help skin heal.

Servings: 1

Ingredients:
2 medium stalks celery
1 handful spinach
4 medium carrots
1 handful parsley
½ medium apple, cored and seeded

Juicer: Follow the instructions for your particular appliance. Refrigerate any unused juice in an airtight container for up to 48 hours.

Blender: Peel and roughly chop all the produce before blending it together, then strain the mixture. Refrigerate any unused juice in an airtight container for up to 48 hours.

Strawberry Hair Shimmer

You can't rely on conditioner alone to keep your hair thick and manageable—your diet also plays a big part. Luckily, this blend has what you need. The vitamin A in carrots works to keep your hair nourished and healthy while cucumbers help promote growth. This mix also contains strawberries, which have been shown to protect your hair from thinning or falling out as well as give it a silky glow. And if that isn't enough, this blend happens to be just as good for your skin and nails.

Servings: 2

Ingredients:
2 medium stalks celery
12 medium strawberries, stemmed
2 medium carrots
1 medium cucumber
1 medium red apple, cored and seeded

Juicer: Follow the instructions for your particular appliance. Refrigerate any unused juice in an airtight container for up to 48 hours.

Blender: Peel and roughly chop all the produce before blending it together, then strain the mixture. Refrigerate any unused juice in an airtight container for up to 48 hours.

BLOOD SUGAR

High Blood Sugar Blend

If keeping your blood sugar in check is important to you, juicing at home is the only way to go. Bottled blends are often low in nutrients and high in added sugars to make them palatable. But in the comfort of your own kitchen, you can make sure your juice blend is delicious *and* has all the right stuff—plenty of vegetables, few sugary fruits, and nothing you don't need.

Servings: 2

Ingredients:
2 medium stalks celery
4 handfuls spinach
1 large carrot
1 medium green apple, cored and seeded
1 small cucumber

Juicer: Follow the instructions for your particular appliance. Refrigerate any unused juice in an airtight container for up to 48 hours.

Blender: Peel and roughly chop all the produce before blending it together, then strain the mixture. Refrigerate any unused juice in an airtight container for up to 48 hours.

Low Blood Sugar Blend

If you struggle with low blood sugar, refined sugar can leave you drained. But a glass of homemade juice may be the perfect pick-me-up. A little bit of the natural sugar in fruit juice combined with celery and leafy greens helps energize you for the long haul. The next time your blood sugar gets a little low, skip the candy bar and grab a glass of this juice blend instead.

Servings: 2

Ingredients:
4 large stalks celery
1 medium cucumber
4 cups spinach
2 medium oranges, peeled
1 medium apple, cored and seeded
1 medium lemon, peeled

Juicer: Follow the instructions for your particular appliance. Refrigerate any unused juice in an airtight container for up to 48 hours.

Blender: Peel and roughly chop all the produce before blending it together, then strain the mixture. Refrigerate any unused juice in an airtight container for up to 48 hours.

Cucumber-Cilantro Delight

Even though it's all natural, fruit can be tricky for people with high blood sugar. Some fruits are fine in moderation, while others (bananas, pineapple, and mango, to name a few) can cause blood-sugar spikes. One sure-fire way of keeping your sugar intake down is to skip the fruit altogether with a veggie-heavy blend like this one.

Servings: 1

Ingredients:
2 medium stalks celery
1 medium orange or red bell pepper, cored and seeded
½ large cucumber
1 handful spinach
1 medium carrot
½ bunch cilantro
Juice of 1 medium lime

Juicer: Follow the instructions for your particular appliance, stirring the lime juice into the finished mixture. Refrigerate any unused juice in an airtight container for up to 48 hours.

Blender: Peel and roughly chop all the produce before blending it together, then strain the mixture. Stir the lime juice into the finished juice. Refrigerate any unused juice in an airtight container for up to 48 hours.

BONE HEALTH

Lemon-Broccoli Bone Defense

Keeping your bones strong and healthy is all about getting the right nutrition. This simple calcium-rich blend can get you well on your way. While acidic foods can leach calcium from your body, the alkalizing properties of cucumber and celery will help balance any acidity and maintain bone density.

Servings: 1

Ingredients:
4 medium stalks celery
1 medium cucumber
½ head broccoli
Juice of ¼ medium lemon

Juicer: Follow the instructions for your particular appliance, stirring the lemon juice into the finished mixture. Refrigerate any unused juice in an airtight container for up to 48 hours.

Blender: Peel and roughly chop all the produce before blending it together, then strain the mixture. Stir the lemon juice into the finished juice. Refrigerate any unused juice in an airtight container for up to 48 hours.

Tropical Strength

In addition to making any green juice deliciously sweet, a serving of pineapple packs in 75 percent of your recommended daily intake of manganese, a mineral that's essential in developing strong bones. Add that to the bone-building properties of celery, cucumber, and spinach, and you have a blend that's as powerful as it is tasty.

Servings: 1

Ingredients:
2 large stalks celery
1½ cups cubed pineapple
1 cup loosely packed spinach
½ cup chopped cucumber
1 (1-inch) piece ginger, peeled
Juice of 1 medium lime

Juicer: Follow the instructions for your particular appliance, stirring the lime juice into the finished mixture. Refrigerate any unused juice in an airtight container for up to 48 hours.

Blender: Peel and roughly chop all the produce before blending it together, then strain the mixture. Stir the lime juice into the finished juice. Refrigerate any unused juice in an airtight container for up to 48 hours.

Apple-Beet Calcium Supercharge

Sure, a cold glass of milk is refreshing, but it may not be as healthy a juice as the right green juice. This calcium-rich juice blend packs in not only calcium but also bone-strengthening manganese and vitamin K. It's also great for your brain, your heart, and your immune system. Make this mix a part of your regular routine to keep your body healthy *and* strong.

Servings: 2

Ingredients:
8 medium stalks celery
3 small red beets
1 handful kale
1 cup broccoli florets
¼ cup chopped parsley
2 medium apples, cored and seeded

Juicer: Follow the instructions for your particular appliance. Refrigerate any unused juice in an airtight container for up to 48 hours.

Blender: Peel and roughly chop all the produce before blending it together, then strain the mixture. Refrigerate any unused juice in an airtight container for up to 48 hours.

BRAIN HEALTH

Blueberry Boost

The blueberries in this recipe (with the help of a bit of red beet) are brimming with antioxidants that help improve cognitive function and reduce cellular aging. They also improve oxygenated blood flow to the brain, which helps prevent neurodegenerative disorders. Sip this sweet, beautifully colored blend while working on your daily crossword puzzle to keep your brain in tip-top shape.

Servings: 2

Ingredients:
2 medium stalks celery
1 cup blueberries
1 medium apple, cored and seeded
½ small cucumber
¼ medium red beet
Juice of ¼ medium lemon or lime
½ cup water

Juicer: Follow the instructions for your particular appliance, stirring the lemon or lime juice and water into the finished mixture. Refrigerate any unused juice in an airtight container for up to 48 hours.

Blender: Peel and roughly chop all the produce before blending it together, then strain the mixture. Stir the lemon or lime juice and water into the finished juice. Refrigerate any unused juice in an airtight container for up to 48 hours.

Morning Jump-Start

Skip the coffee run and reach for this energizing juice instead to jump-start your cognitive function first thing in the morning (or during the afternoon slump). The beets are the star in this blend, getting your blood pumping and moving more oxygen to your brain when you need it most.

Servings: 1

Ingredients:
2 medium stalks celery
2 medium red beets
1 medium carrot
1 medium green apple, cored and seeded
½ medium lemon, peeled
1 (1-inch) piece ginger, peeled

Juicer: Follow the instructions for your particular appliance. Refrigerate any unused juice in an airtight container for up to 48 hours.

Blender: Peel and roughly chop all the produce before blending it together, then strain the mixture. Refrigerate any unused juice in an airtight container for up to 48 hours.

Cucumber-Kale Oxygen Boost

If you want your brain to fire on all cylinders, you need to make sure your whole body is getting the nutrition it needs. This blend harnesses the powers of celery and kale to improve blood flow and allow more oxygen to reach your brain. The antioxidants in the vegetables tackle oxidative stress that can lead to degenerative illnesses, such as Alzheimer's.

Servings: 3

Ingredients:
1 bunch celery
½ bunch cilantro
I handful kale
1 medium cucumber
1 lemon, peeled
1 lime, peeled
1 (1-inch) piece ginger, peeled

Juicer: Follow the instructions for your particular appliance. Refrigerate any unused juice in an airtight container for up to 48 hours.

Blender: Peel and roughly chop all the produce before blending it together, then strain the mixture. Refrigerate any unused juice in an airtight container for up to 48 hours.

DIGESTION

Sweet and Spicy Tonic

Don't let the name throw you off—this isn't the sort of spicy that will make stomach troubles worse. Ginger and turmeric give this sweet green juice a powerful bite that can help treat all manner of digestive issues, including nausea, indigestion, and constipation. Plus, pineapple helps speed the digestive process to keep bloat at bay. This is a great juice to add to your regular regimen to maintain healthy digestion and a flat stomach.

Servings: 2

Ingredients:
2 medium stalks celery
1 medium pineapple, peeled and cored
1 (2-inch) piece ginger, peeled
1 (3-inch) piece turmeric, peeled
1–2 medium apples, cored and seeded
Juice of 2 medium limes

Juicer: Follow the instructions for your particular appliance. Then strain the juice using a fine-mesh strainer or cheesecloth to remove the remaining fiber so the juice is easier to digest. Stir the lime juice into the finished mixture. Refrigerate any unused juice in an airtight container for up to 48 hours.

Blender: Peel and roughly chop all the produce before blending it together, then strain the mixture. Stir the lime juice into the finished juice. Refrigerate any unused juice in an airtight container for up to 48 hours.

NOTE: If you suffer from irritable bowel syndrome, make sure you substitute more celery or pineapple for the apples, which can be an IBS trigger.

Apple-Fennel Stomach Soother

Thanks to a healthy dose of fennel, this simple recipe can help relieve gas, bloating, constipation, and diarrhea. The pectin-based polysaccharides in celery can also help soothe an upset stomach, making this a great go-to recipe whenever yours starts to rumble.

Servings: 1

Ingredients:
2 medium stalks celery
2 medium bulbs fennel
1–2 medium apples, cored and seeded
1 medium lime, peeled

Juicer: Follow the instructions for your particular appliance. Then strain the juice using a fine-mesh strainer or cheesecloth to remove the remaining fiber so the juice is easier to digest. Refrigerate any unused juice in an airtight container for up to 48 hours.

Blender: Peel and roughly chop all the produce before blending it together, then strain the mixture. Refrigerate any unused juice in an airtight container for up to 48 hours.

Ginger-Mint Tummy Tonic

This juice packs in everything you need to keep your stomach running smoothly *and* treat any digestive troubles: celery and lime detoxify, cucumber and ginger soothe, and fennel relieves. Mint not only adds a refreshing touch but also has stomach-soothing properties of its own. But you may want to leave it out if you suffer from heartburn or acid reflux, which mint can worsen.

Servings: 2

Ingredients:
4 large stalks celery
1 medium cucumber
½ bulb fennel
1 large apple, cored and seeded
1 medium lime, peeled
1 handful mint
1 (1-inch) piece ginger, peeled

Juicer: Follow the instructions for your particular appliance. Then strain the juice using a fine-mesh strainer or cheesecloth to remove the remaining fiber so the juice is easier to digest. Refrigerate any unused juice in an airtight container for up to 48 hours.

Blender: Peel and roughly chop all the produce before blending it together, then strain the mixture. Refrigerate any unused juice in an airtight container for up to 48 hours.

HEART HEALTH

Carrot-Ginger Gym Buddy

One small, red beet can make a big difference when it comes to your heart health. Not only can beets help lower blood pressure and prevent heart disease when consumed regularly, but they can also make it easier to get your exercise, which is great for your heart. When you eat (or drink) beets two to three hours before physical activity, they can help improve oxygen use and keep you from tiring out too soon.

Servings: 1

Ingredients:
2 medium stalks celery
1 small red beet
1 large apple, cored and seeded
1–2 small carrots
½ medium lemon or lime, peeled
1 (½-inch) piece ginger, peeled

Juicer: Follow the instructions for your particular appliance. Refrigerate any unused juice in an airtight container for up to 48 hours.

Blender: Peel and roughly chop all the produce before blending it together, then strain the mixture. Refrigerate any unused juice in an airtight container for up to 48 hours.

Cucumber-Spinach Heart Hero

If you've experienced heart failure (or want to prevent it), studies show that you can't do any better than beet juice. That's because of the nitrates in beet juice—as well as in celery and spinach—that increase oxygen in the blood and strengthen weak muscles. This blend packs in all three, plus some tasty and beneficial extras, for maximum effect.

Servings: 2

Ingredients:
2 medium stalks celery
2 large handfuls spinach
1 medium lemon, peeled
1 (1-inch) piece ginger, peeled
1 large carrot
1 large red beet, with greens
½ medium cucumber
1 medium green apple, cored and seeded (optional)

Juicer: Follow the instructions for your particular appliance. Refrigerate any unused juice in an airtight container for up to 48 hours.

Blender: Peel and roughly chop all the produce before blending it together, then strain the mixture. Refrigerate any unused juice in an airtight container for up to 48 hours.

Berry Blood Pressure Blend

While beets are the best for lowering blood pressure, not everyone loves their earthy taste. The berries in this blend, which are themselves full of heart-healthy antioxidants, keep things sweet and refreshing. If you're not a fan of ginger, feel free to leave it out. But studies show this root is also beneficial for lowering blood pressure.

Servings: 4

Ingredients:
4 medium stalks celery
7 medium carrots
1 pound strawberries, stemmed
½ pint blueberries
1 large red beet
1 (1-inch) piece ginger, peeled

Juicer: Follow the instructions for your particular appliance. Refrigerate any unused juice in an airtight container for up to 48 hours.

Blender: Peel and roughly chop all the produce before blending it together, then strain the mixture. Refrigerate any unused juice in an airtight container for up to 48 hours.

HYDRATION

Apple-Pear Refresher

It's not hard to stay hydrated when you add juicing to your routine—fruits and vegetables are mostly water, after all. This simple recipe whips up quickly, making it easier for you to stay quenched throughout your day. Reach for it to replace the hydration you've lost when you first roll out of bed, when you get back from the gym, or when you've spent too long in the sun.

Servings: 1

Ingredients:
3 medium stalks celery
½ medium cucumber
1 medium green apple, cored and seeded
1 medium pear, cored and seeded

Juicer: Follow the instructions for your particular appliance. Refrigerate any unused juice in an airtight container for up to 48 hours.

Blender: Peel and roughly chop all the produce before blending it together, then strain the mixture. Refrigerate any unused juice in an airtight container for up to 48 hours.

Green Lemonade

There's nothing better than a cold glass of lemonade on a warm day, but the summer staple has 25 grams of sugar in just one glass! This blend has a trick up its sleeve: all the nutrients and hydration your body needs *plus* that sweet-and-tart flavor your taste buds crave with no added sugar. You can finish off your juice with another squeeze of lemon and maybe a bit of honey, depending on how you like your lemonade.

Servings: 2

Ingredients:
4 medium stalks celery
1 small cucumber
2 cups chopped spinach
2 cups chopped kale
1 medium green apple, cored and seeded
½ large lemon, peeled

Juicer: Follow the instructions for your particular appliance. Refrigerate any unused juice in an airtight container for up to 48 hours.

Blender: Peel and roughly chop all the produce before blending it together, then strain the mixture. Refrigerate any unused juice in an airtight container for up to 48 hours.

Cucumber Hydration

While it's important to drink enough water in a day, it can be easier said than done—especially if you prefer beverages with a little more flavor. Each of the ingredients in this sweet blend (besides the mint) has a water content of 90 percent or above, not to mention plenty of vitamins and minerals to keep you feeling great. Grab a glass when you need to break up the hydration monotony.

Servings: 3

Ingredients:
2 medium stalks celery
2–3 large cucumbers
2 medium apples, cored and seeded
1 handful medium strawberries, stemmed
Mint, to taste

Juicer: Follow the instructions for your particular appliance. Refrigerate any unused juice in an airtight container for up to 48 hours.

Blender: Peel and roughly chop all the produce before blending it together, then strain the mixture. Refrigerate any unused juice in an airtight container for up to 48 hours.

Headache Blend

Headaches are a common symptom with any number of causes, one of which is dehydration. A tall glass of water should be your first line of defense when you feel a headache coming on. But if that doesn't work, it's time to try this blend. It provides not just hydration but also electrolytes, antioxidants, anti-inflammatory compounds, magnesium, potassium, and calcium—all of which can help combat a headache. Give it a try before you reach for the pain relievers and you may not need them.

Servings: 1

Ingredients:
2 medium stalks celery
2 leaves Swiss chard, with stems
¼ medium pineapple, peeled and cored
1 large handful spinach
1 medium cucumber
1 medium lemon, peeled
1 (1-inch) piece ginger, peeled

Juicer: Follow the instructions for your particular appliance. Refrigerate any unused juice in an airtight container for up to 48 hours.

Blender: Peel and roughly chop all the produce before blending it together, then strain the mixture. Refrigerate any unused juice in an airtight container for up to 48 hours.

IMMUNE HEALTH

Sweet Immunity

An apple a day keeps the doctor away, especially when it's paired with celery, citrus, and ginger. This recipe is best served straight away to preserve all of those immune-boosting nutrients. You can certainly let it chill for an hour or two, but keeping it around for any more than a day will lessen its effectiveness.

Servings: 2

Ingredients:
2 large stalks celery
1 large sweet apple, cored and seeded
1 (1-inch) piece ginger, peeled
1 large orange, peeled
½ large lemon, peeled

Juicer: Follow the instructions for your particular appliance. Refrigerate any unused juice in an airtight container for up to 24 hours.

Blender: Peel and roughly chop all the produce before blending it together, then strain the mixture. Refrigerate any unused juice in an airtight container for up to 24 hours.

Natural Cold Prevention

Upping your intake of vitamin C during cold and flu season isn't a new idea, but it can be a bit counterproductive if you get your vitamin C from sugary bottled juice. This homemade blend is a vitamin C powerhouse, not to mention it has antibacterial and antimicrobial properties. Add it to your winter routine for a regular boost in your immune health. Try swapping out the oranges for grapefruit and the spinach for kale once in a while for a different flavor with the same great benefits.

Servings: 1

Ingredients:
2 medium stalks celery
2 medium oranges, peeled
2 cups chopped spinach
1 (1-inch) piece ginger, peeled

Juicer: Follow the instructions for your particular appliance. Refrigerate any unused juice in an airtight container for up to 48 hours.

Blender: Peel and roughly chop all the produce before blending it together, then strain the mixture. Refrigerate any unused juice in an airtight container for up to 48 hours.

Flu Fighter

When you get hit with the flu or a bad cold, the symptoms can overwhelm you. This blend features immune-bolstering vitamin C, anti-inflammatory properties, a little heat to soothe sore throats, and ginger for upset stomachs. Not only will it help relieve your symptoms, but it'll also give you a much-needed boost of energy. Just be sure to sip it slowly to keep from upsetting an already-rumbling stomach.

Servings: 1

Ingredients:
2 medium stalks celery
1 medium red beet
3 medium carrots
1 medium orange, peeled
½ medium lemon, peeled
1 (2-inch) piece turmeric, peeled
1 (1-inch) piece ginger, peeled
1 pinch cayenne pepper
1 pinch freshly ground black pepper

Juicer: Follow the instructions for your particular appliance, stirring the cayenne pepper and ground pepper into the finished mixture. Refrigerate any unused juice in an airtight container for up to 48 hours.

Blender: Peel and roughly chop all the produce before blending it together, then strain the mixture. Stir the cayenne pepper and ground pepper into the finished mixture. Refrigerate any unused juice in an airtight container for up to 48 hours.

INFLAMMATION

Body-Calming Blend

Reach for this recipe when you're experiencing aches and pains. This sweet and simple juice packs a powerful punch against inflammation—every one of its ingredients carries anti-inflammatory properties. But this blend can also promote healing, pain relief, and restful sleep, meaning you can treat your symptoms while also treating their source.

Servings: 2

Ingredients:
3 large stalks celery
½ small pineapple, peeled and cored
1–2 heads romaine lettuce
1 medium cucumber
1 (1-inch) piece ginger, peeled

Juicer: Follow the instructions for your particular appliance. Refrigerate any unused juice in an airtight container for up to 48 hours.

Blender: Peel and roughly chop all the produce before blending it together, then strain the mixture. Refrigerate any unused juice in an airtight container for up to 48 hours.

Pineapple Cool Down

If you find yourself reaching for an ice pack more often than not, this is the blend to try. The bromelain in pineapple helps calm inflammation from the inside the way ice relieves it from the outside. Plus, a healthy dose of vitamin C and hydration help strengthen your immune system, which can also reduce inflammation. And all of these benefits come in one really tasty package.

Servings: 2

Ingredients:
2 medium stalks celery
2 cups chopped pineapple
1 tablespoon chopped mint leaves
1 cup chopped cucumber
1 jalapeño, seeded
Juice of 1 medium lime

Juicer: Follow the instructions for your particular appliance, stirring the lime juice into the finished mixture. Refrigerate any unused juice in an airtight container for up to 48 hours.

Blender: Peel and roughly chop all the produce before blending it together, then strain the mixture. Stir the lime juice into the finished juice. Refrigerate any unused juice in an airtight container for up to 48 hours.

Ginger Muscle Maintenance

Whether you have a specific complaint or you ache all over, the right combination of fruits and vegetables can go a long way in offering relief. Each of the items in this blend has its own claim to anti-inflammatory fame, from cucumber's cucurbitacin to apple's quercetin. While lemon peel contains the beneficial chemical limonene, it can add a bit of bitterness to a juice drink. So feel free to peel the lemon or add a bit of natural sweetener to the mix if you like.

Servings: 4

Ingredients:
4 medium stalks celery
2 lightly packed cups spinach
2 large cucumbers
½ bunch parsley
2 large apples, cored and seeded
½ lemon, with peel
1 (½-inch) piece ginger, peeled

Juicer: Follow the instructions for your particular appliance. Refrigerate any unused juice in an airtight container for up to 48 hours.

Blender: Peel and roughly chop all the produce before blending it together, then strain the mixture. Refrigerate any unused juice in an airtight container for up to 48 hours.

Sweat Session Recovery

People who put their bodies to work—whether as a weekend warrior or a regular at the gym—need to make sure they're giving their bodies what they need to recover from activity-related inflammation. This blend may be able to help with that. Not only is it packed with anti-inflammatory goodness, but it's also a refreshing thirst quencher. Enjoy it after any sweat session to help your body cool down and rehydrate.

Servings: 4

Ingredients:
1 small bunch celery, without leaves
1 medium cucumber
4–6 tart apples, cored and seeded
1 small handful mint leaves
1 (1-inch) piece ginger, peeled

Juicer: Follow the instructions for your particular appliance. Refrigerate any unused juice in an airtight container for up to 48 hours.

Blender: Peel and roughly chop all the produce before blending it together, then strain the mixture. Refrigerate any unused juice in an airtight container for up to 48 hours.

MOOD

Broccoli & Carrot Anxiety Ally

If your nerves are getting the better of you, a sip of this blend may be able to help. It contains spinach, which (thanks to magnesium and tryptophan) can boost your mood, relax your muscles and nerves, and help you sleep. Celery adds even more calming power by lowering the stress hormones in your blood, while broccoli's folate helps fend off depression. If you're not wild about the earthy flavor, try adding a bit of honey or a splash of lemon juice to the mix.

Servings: 2

Ingredients:
4 medium stalks celery
2 large handfuls spinach
3–4 medium stalks broccoli
1 large carrot

Juicer: Follow the instructions for your particular appliance. Refrigerate any unused juice in an airtight container for up to 48 hours.

Blender: Peel and roughly chop all the produce before blending it together, then strain the mixture. Refrigerate any unused juice in an airtight container for up to 48 hours.

WEIGHT LOSS

Parsley Digestif

One of the best ways to encourage weight loss is to make sure your body is getting what it needs to keep your digestive system humming along. Celery, cucumber, and leafy greens help keep things moving, while a hint of sweetness makes this a recipe you'll reach for regularly.

Servings: 1

Ingredients:
2 medium stalks celery
⅓ small cucumber
1 cup trimmed kale
1 cup baby spinach
3 sprigs parsley
¼ medium green apple, cored and seeded
Juice of ¼ medium lemon

Juicer: Follow the instructions for your particular appliance, stirring the lemon juice into the finished mixture. Refrigerate any unused juice in an airtight container for up to 48 hours.

Blender: Peel and roughly chop all the produce before blending it together, then strain the mixture. Stir the lemon juice into the finished juice. Refrigerate any unused juice in an airtight container for up to 48 hours.

Apple-Cinnamon Soother

Making the change to a healthy diet can be hard, especially if you have a sweet tooth. But drinking celery-based juices can actually help you curb sugar cravings while sticking to your wellness plan. This particular blend adds apples and cinnamon for a distinctly dessert-like flavor. Whip it up when you need a little something sweet.

Servings: 1

Ingredients:
8 medium stalks celery
2 large apples, cored and seeded
1 dash ground cinnamon

Juicer: Follow the instructions for your particular appliance, stirring the cinnamon into the finished mixture. Refrigerate any unused juice in an airtight container for up to 48 hours.

Blender: Peel and roughly chop all the produce before blending it together, then strain the mixture. Stir the cinnamon into the finished juice. Refrigerate any unused juice in an airtight container for up to 48 hours.

Strawberry-Apple Good Start

Although you want to try to steer clear of sugary fruits when juicing for weight loss, a little sweetness can go a long way toward making this healthy change more palatable. If you're just starting out or you're not crazy about more earthy juices, give this blend a try. All of the produce is high in water content and fiber (as well as essential nutrients), which helps your digestive system function at its best. Just be sure to work some vegetable-rich juices into your routine, too.

Servings: 3

Ingredients:
6 medium stalks celery
4 medium carrots
1 medium cucumber
1 medium green apple, cored and seeded
4 medium strawberries, stemmed
1 (1-inch) piece ginger, peeled

Juicer: Follow the instructions for your particular appliance. Refrigerate any unused juice in an airtight container for up to 48 hours.

Blender: Peel and roughly chop all the produce before blending it together, then strain the mixture. Refrigerate any unused juice in an airtight container for up to 48 hours.

Nourishing Pear Detox

When you start a new diet or wellness routine, it can be difficult to make sure your body's getting everything it needs. This blend is here to help you stay hydrated, clear out lingering toxins, and fill in any nutritional holes. While superfood kale is like an all-natural multivitamin, not everyone loves the way it tastes. So, detoxifying pear and celery sweeten the blend while mint adds a refreshing touch (and soothes any stomach upset resulting from dietary changes).

Servings: 1

Ingredients:
2 medium stalks celery
6 medium pears, cored and seeded
3 cups chopped kale
2 tablespoons chopped fresh mint

Juicer: Follow the instructions for your particular appliance. Refrigerate any unused juice in an airtight container for up to 48 hours.

Blender: Peel and roughly chop all the produce before blending it together, then strain the mixture. Refrigerate any unused juice in an airtight container for up to 48 hours.

WHOLE BODY WELLNESS

The Kitchen Sink

Throwing everything but the kitchen sink into a juicer is certainly one way to get all the vitamins and minerals your body needs! This recipe packs in a variety of healthful ingredients that balances out both flavor and nutrients. The end result is a tasty blend that will help you feel your best.

Servings: 2

Ingredients:
4 large stalks celery
2 cups chopped kale
1 large green apple, cored and seeded
1 cup chopped pineapple
½ cup chopped parsley
1 tablespoon chopped mint
1 medium cucumber
1 (1-inch) piece ginger, peeled
Juice of 1 medium lemon

Juicer: Follow the instructions for your particular appliance, stirring the lemon juice into the finished mixture. Refrigerate any unused juice in an airtight container for up to 48 hours.

Blender: Peel and roughly chop all the produce before blending it together, then strain the mixture. Stir the lemon juice into the finished juice. Refrigerate any unused juice in an airtight container for up to 48 hours.

The Multivitamin

Whether you're feeling a little bit drained or you're just looking to maintain your good health, this blend is sure to put some pep in your step. It provides an always appreciated boost in sustainable energy as well as the vitamins and minerals to maintain your bone, brain, heart, immune, *and* eye health. This is a great blend to reach for when you're looking to restore your body's natural balance.

Servings: 2

Ingredients:
5 medium stalks celery
1 medium red beet, with greens
8–10 medium carrots
1 lemon, peeled
1 lime, peeled
1 (½-inch) piece ginger, peeled
1 (½-inch) piece turmeric, peeled

Juicer: Follow the instructions for your particular appliance. Refrigerate any unused juice in an airtight container for up to 48 hours.

Blender: Peel and roughly chop all the produce before blending it together, then strain the mixture. Refrigerate any unused juice in an airtight container for up to 48 hours.

Better Than V8

Bottled juice is great in concept—it's done for you, delicious, and ready to travel. But too many of the juices you see in the store have lost a lot of their nutritional content and replaced it with way too much sugar and sodium. This nutrient-packed blend might take a little effort, but the fresh flavor it delivers will be worth it.

Servings: 2

Ingredients:
2 large stalks celery
3 medium tomatoes
1 large carrot
½ medium cucumber
1 leaf kale
1 handful watercress
1 handful parsley
1 medium radish
½ medium red beet
1 spear broccoli
Worcestershire sauce, to taste

Juicer: Follow the instructions for your particular appliance, stirring the Worcestershire sauce into the finished mixture. Refrigerate any unused juice in an airtight container for up to 48 hours.

Blender: Peel and roughly chop all the produce before blending it together, then strain the mixture. Stir the Worcestershire sauce into the finished juice. Refrigerate any unused juice in an airtight container for up to 48 hours.

Sunshine in a Cup

Citrus fruits can not only boost your mood but also protect your heart, help you maintain your blood sugar, support your immune system and shorten a cold, lower your risk of stroke, give you glowing skin, *and* help you absorb other nutrients. And if that isn't enough, they also taste great. You can't really ask more than that of a juice!

Servings: 1

Ingredients:
1 medium stalk celery
1 cup chopped spinach
2 medium lemons, peeled
1 medium lime, peeled
2 medium oranges, peeled

Juicer: Follow the instructions for your particular appliance. Refrigerate any unused juice in an airtight container for up to 48 hours.

Blender: Peel and roughly chop all the produce before blending it together, then strain the mixture. Refrigerate any unused juice in an airtight container for up to 48 hours.

Celery Smoothies

Juicing isn't the only way to make the most of celery's many nutrients. Adding smoothies to your juicing repertoire can help quell dietary boredom, up your intake of beneficial veggies and fruits, and introduce even more healthy ingredients into your wellness routine. While making a smoothie is a little different than making juice, it's just as straightforward and rewarding.

The most important thing to note is that, with smoothies, you don't strain anything out. That means that you get *all* of the nutrients that the flesh of each ingredient has to offer. It also means that you shouldn't put anything into the blender that you don't want to drink. You'll remove the peels, so you do lose any of the nutrients contained there. But you benefit from all of the fiber, which can help regulate your digestive system, lower cholesterol levels, control blood sugar levels, and help you maintain a healthy weight.

While both juices and smoothies are a great way of getting your recommended amount of fruits and veggies, smoothies have a handy advantage. With juices, the purer the end product, the better, because you want that thirst-quenching juice consistency. But smoothies are made to be thick and creamy, which means you can round out your blend with all sorts of extras. You'll see recipes call for protein powder, spices, extracts, nut milks, and coconut products, plus yogurt, chia seeds, flax seeds, oats, chopped nuts, and more.

These additions are a great way to supplement your diet. Need a breakfast you can take to go? A peanut butter oatmeal smoothie (made with frozen bananas) could do the trick. Hair and nails need a pick-me-up? Add some flaxseed to your blend. Looking to add a hint of flavor and boost nutrients without adding calories? Swap your plain water for coconut water. The bottom line is that smoothies are a great way to get even more nutritional benefits in a quick and convenient beverage.

But just like juices, smoothies aren't meant to replace your meals. You can sub one in in a pinch (breakfast to go, for example), but smoothies are just one nutritional tool in your wellness belt. Your body still needs plenty of healthy solid food to function. And with all of those extras, calorie counts can creep up. So just make sure you're not undoing all of your hard detox work while experimenting with tasty blends.

Ready to get started? Adding smoothies to your routine is easy—all you need is a high-speed blender and a good knife. To make a great smoothie, keep these tips in mind:

- **Prep your produce.** Unless "frozen" is indicated in the recipe, start with fresh, organic ingredients. You'll need to peel your produce, including ginger and turmeric, remove any cores and seeds, and roughly chop everything before blending. You should also remove anything you, personally, don't want to drink. If the strings on celery bug you, pull them off before adding the celery to the mix.
- **Blend it well.** Blend your ingredients one or two at a time on high to avoid any chunks ending up in the bottom of your glass. Add ice, frozen fruit, water, or other liquids (think almond milk or coconut water) to get the consistency and flavor you want.
- **Make any recipe your own.** If you don't love what's listed in the ingredients, feel free to substitute any green with another green or any fruit with another fruit. That way, you maintain the blend's balance. Then taste the finished product and adjust accordingly, adding more fruit if the blend is bitter or more lemon if you like it tart, for example.
- **Drink it fresh.** If you store your smoothie for later, make sure you shake or stir it before drinking it. You can refrigerate a smoothie for up to 48 hours, or freeze it indefinitely without losing any nutrients. (Like juice ice pops, smoothie ice pops are a great option!)

To get you started, here are ten simple smoothie recipes with wonderful health benefits. These blends are all green, meaning they're focused on fruits and vegetables with few additions. That's to help you transition into smoothie territory, easily incorporating these blends into your juicing routine. But when it comes to smoothies, the sky's the limit. So start here and then use this information as a springboard to create your own nutritious and delicious blends.

The Classic Green Smoothie

When you picture a smoothie, you might imagine a creamy yellow or pink drink garnished with a slice of pineapple or a strawberry. But this blend takes the humble fruit smoothie to a new level of nourishing. Think of it as the smoothie version of super-healthy green juice—still fruity but also packed with veggie goodness.

Servings: 4

Ingredients:
1 cup chopped celery
1 cup chopped kale
1 (½-inch) piece ginger
2 medium oranges
½ medium lemon
1 small frozen banana
1 cup frozen peaches
1 cup cold water
1 cup ice

Peel, seed, core, and roughly chop all the whole ingredients before adding them to a blender. Blend ingredients one or two at a time on high speed until the mixture is smooth. Enjoy immediately or refrigerate the smoothie for up to 24 hours.

Antioxidant Blend

This colorful blend is a great way to introduce your friends and family (or maybe yourself) to juicing. The fruity flavor tricks your brain into thinking you're having a treat, but this smoothie packs a nutritious punch. It's full of antioxidants, which help neutralize free radicals and prevent chronic illness and disease.

Servings: 4

Ingredients:
2 medium stalks celery
1 large apple
1 (1-inch) piece ginger
Juice of 1 medium lime
1 medium frozen banana
1 cup blueberries
2 cups coconut water

Peel, seed, core, and roughly chop all the whole ingredients before adding them to a blender. Blend ingredients one or two at a time on high speed until the mixture is smooth. Enjoy immediately or refrigerate the smoothie for up to 24 hours.

Tropical Detox

Who knew that getting the right nutrition could be so delightful? This flavorful blend has everything you need to reset your digestive system, from healing antioxidants to detoxifying fiber and anti-inflammatory enzymes. Make the most of this act of self-care by enjoying your smoothie outside in the sunshine on a warm day (tiny umbrella optional).

Servings: 4

Ingredients:
2 medium stalks celery
1 cup chopped pineapple
1 medium cucumber
1 medium lemon
1 (1-inch) piece ginger
1 cup chopped frozen banana
1 (10-ounce) bag frozen peach slices
2 cups ice

Peel, seed, core, and roughly chop all the whole ingredients before adding them to a blender. Blend ingredients one or two at a time on high speed until the mixture is smooth. Enjoy immediately or refrigerate the smoothie for up to 24 hours.

Heart-Smart Smoothie

This recipe may not look like much, but it is chock-full of heart-healthy potassium, vitamin K, and antioxidants. These nutrients can help lower your blood pressure and cholesterol while also supporting bone health. And because it's as delicious as it is beneficial, adding this smoothie to your routine is one heart-healthy change you won't mind making.

Servings: 4

Ingredients:
6 large stalks celery
1–2 medium fresh or frozen bananas
1–2 cups frozen blueberries
10–16 ounces coconut water

Peel, seed, core, and roughly chop all the whole ingredients before adding them to a blender. Blend ingredients one or two at a time on high speed until the mixture is smooth. Enjoy immediately or refrigerate the smoothie for up to 24 hours.

Anti-Inflammatory Blend

Inflammation is the body's response to injury, and it's usually a good thing; it tells your immune system to start the healing process. But if it goes on too long, it can lead to things like heart disease or even cancer. Blends like this one may be able to help protect the body from damage. Between the bromelain in pineapple, the phytonutrients in cucumber, and the vitamin C in celery and lime, this smoothie offers some powerful relief from inflammation.

Servings: 2

Ingredients:
1 cup chopped celery
2 cups frozen chopped pineapple
2 cups peeled and chopped cucumber
2 tablespoons chopped fresh basil
2 teaspoons lime juice
1 cup water
1 pinch salt
½ cup ice
Celery stalk, for garnish

Peel, seed, core, and roughly chop all the whole ingredients before adding them to a blender. Blend ingredients one or two at a time on high speed until the mixture is smooth. Enjoy immediately, garnished with a celery stalk, or refrigerate the smoothie for up to 24 hours.

Banana-Berry Blood-Sugar Blend

Smoothies have a solid advantage over juice where blood sugar is concerned. Rather than distilling fruit into a sugary concentrate, smoothies contain the whole fruit with all of its fiber, which helps control blood sugar levels. And berries, in particular, have actually been shown to protect your cells from high blood sugar and increase sensitivity to insulin. So you can feel good about adding this blood sugar–friendly blend to your wellness routine (in moderation, of course).

Servings: 2

Ingredients:
5 medium stalks celery
2 medium bananas
1 medium red apple
1 cup water
1 cup frozen strawberries
1 cup frozen raspberries

Peel, seed, core, and roughly chop all the whole ingredients before adding them to a blender. Blend ingredients one or two at a time on high speed until the mixture is smooth. Enjoy immediately or refrigerate the smoothie for up to 24 hours.

Glowing Skin Smoothie

The best way to get glowing skin is by working from the inside out. Not only is this delicious smoothie full of skin-loving antioxidants, but it can also help lower breakout-causing stress levels, remove toxins, and give you a boost of hydration. Once your body is getting the nutrients it needs, you may find that you can simplify your skin care routine.

Servings: 3

Ingredients:
3 medium stalks celery
1 head romaine lettuce
1 cup chopped spinach
1 medium banana
1 medium green apple
1 medium peach
¼ cup chopped cilantro
½ medium lemon
½ cup water

Peel, seed, core, and roughly chop all the whole ingredients before adding them to a blender. Blend ingredients one or two at a time on high speed until the mixture is smooth. Enjoy immediately or refrigerate the smoothie for up to 24 hours.

Bloat Banisher

The best way to combat belly bloat is to support your digestive system with hydration, good nutrition, a healthy amount of fiber, and, occasionally, digestive enzymes to help move things along. Pineapple and papaya both contain these types of enzymes while the green ingredients in this blend help with the rest of the digestive checklist. Smoothies like this one are a great addition to your juicing roster. Just don't go overboard—too much fiber can *cause* bloating.

Servings: 2

Ingredients:
2 medium stalks celery
2 cups chopped spinach
1 large cucumber
2 cups frozen chopped pineapple
½ cup fresh or frozen cubed papaya
1 tablespoon grated ginger
1 tablespoon lime juice

Peel, seed, core, and roughly chop all the whole ingredients before adding them to a blender. Blend ingredients one or two at a time on high speed until the mixture is smooth. Enjoy immediately or refrigerate the smoothie for up to 24 hours.

Energizing Blend

If you like to have a smoothie for breakfast or as an afternoon treat, this is the perfect blend for you. It's full of essential nutrients, antioxidants, and B vitamins that can give you a more sustained energy boost than a cup of coffee. And while coffee is a delicious pick-me-up, it doesn't also support your heart health, immune system, bone density, cognitive function, and digestive system the way that the right smoothie does. Try starting your day with a glass of this simple mix and you're sure to feel the difference.

Servings: 2

Ingredients:
1 medium stalk celery
2 cups chopped spinach
2 (2-inch-thick) slices fresh pineapple, including core
2 cups almond milk

Peel, seed, core, and roughly chop all the whole ingredients before adding them to a blender. Blend ingredients one or two at a time on high speed until the mixture is smooth. Enjoy immediately or refrigerate the smoothie for up to 24 hours.

Immune Booster

Whether you're feeling under the weather or you're trying to escape flu season unscathed, this antioxidant-rich blend is what you need. Mango is a multitasker: not only does it sweeten this blend and bolster your immune system with vitamin C, but it's also been shown to improve brain function, brighten skin, aid digestion, and help you lose weight. Add this mix to a well-balanced diet (and maybe avoid direct contact with doorknobs) to keep your immune system in tip-top shape.

Servings: 2

Ingredients:
1 cup chopped celery
1 cup chopped spinach
¼ cup chopped parsley
2 cups water
1 medium cucumber
1 (½-inch) piece ginger
3 cups frozen chopped mango
Juice of 1 medium lemon

Peel, seed, core, and roughly chop all the whole ingredients before adding them to a blender. Blend ingredients one or two at a time on high speed until the mixture is smooth. Enjoy immediately or refrigerate the smoothie for up to 24 hours.

Conversion Chart

Metric and Imperial Conversions

(These conversions are rounded for convenience.)

Ingredient	Cups/ Tablespoons/ Teaspoons	Ounces	Grams/ Milliliters
Fruit, dried	1 cup	4 ounces	120 grams
Fruits or veggies, chopped	1 cup	5 to 7 ounces	145 to 200 grams
Fruits or veggies, puréed	1 cup	8.5 ounces	245 grams
Honey, maple syrup, or corn syrup	1 tablespoon	0.75 ounce	20 grams
Liquids: cream, milk, water, or juice	1 cup	8 fluid ounces	240 milliliters
Salt	1 teaspoon	0.2 ounces	6 grams
Spices: cinnamon, cloves, ginger, or nutmeg (ground)	1 teaspoon	0.2 ounce	5 milliliters
Sugar, brown, firmly packed	1 cup	7 ounces	200 grams
Sugar, white	1 cup/ 1 tablespoon	7 ounces/0.5 ounce	200 grams/12.5 grams
Vanilla extract	1 teaspoon	0.2 ounce	4 grams

Liquids

8 fluid ounces = 1 cup = ½ pint
16 fluid ounces = 2 cups = 1 pint
32 fluid ounces = 4 cups = 1 quart
128 fluid ounces = 16 cups = 1 gallon

Index

About the Author

Annie Willis is passionate about health and wellness. After years of poor health and exhaustion, she found relief in whole, healthy foods and fell in love with preparing them at home. Annie lives in Colorado with her husband and their two Pomeranians, Olive and Basil.